fearfully and wonderfully broken

Fighting for Faith When You're Falling Apart

SYDNEY ANNE BENNETT

W Publishing Group

An Imprint of Thomas Nelson

Fearfully and Wonderfully Broken

Published by W Publishing, an imprint of Thomas Nelson, 501 Nelson Place, Nashville, TN 37214, USA.

The author is represented by Alive Literary Agency, www.aliveliterary.com.

Thomas Nelson titles may be purchased in bulk for educational, business, fundraising, or sales promotional use. For information, please email SpecialMarkets@ThomasNelson.com.

ISBN 978-1-4003-5051-3 (audiobook)
ISBN 978-1-4003-2050-6 (ePub)
ISBN 978-1-4003-5049-0 (softcover)

HarperCollins Publishers, Macken House, 39/40 Mayor Street Upper, Dublin 1, D01 C9W8, Ireland (https://www.harpercollins.com).

Names of some individuals have been changed to preserve their privacy.

Library of Congress Control Number: 2025951536

Art Direction: Meg Schmidt
Cover Design: Faceout Studio
Interior Design: Sara Colley

Printed in the United States of America

26 27 28 29 30 LBC 5 4 3 2 1

To Colton, the love of my life.
Until We Rise.

contents

Part Three: Daughter

PART ONE

disability

ONE

butterfly

I need to write this book because I'm in pain. Perhaps one day I'll discover I was in pain because I needed to write this book. It seems in every battle of my life, I have first tried to fight all on my own. This battle with pain is no different. For weeks I've read short sections of Scripture, but when I try to pray, the words won't come. I have dried up inside. I am angry. And I don't even know what—or who—I am angry at. I pray, when I am able, that God will make me want to pray. And the pain keeps getting worse.

Right now the pain is in my arm, curling the tips of my fingers as I type, sometimes crossing over to the other side of my body through invisible threads, nerve to plaintive nerve, communicating tiny, wicked signals through space, shooting at times down my core, my back, my ribs, my legs, and up my throat. A schizophrenia of pain. Undecided, except to hurt. Some things are just allowed to be, it seems. Sometimes the things that most require justification for existing, just exist.

Madeleine L'Engle wrote, "Someone has altered the script. / My lines have been changed. / The other actors are shifting roles."[1] The other actors aren't the playwright. They're secondary causes, a step down from the playwright but still crucial to the plot. Secondary causes like chemo lead to the loss of hair. Secondary causes like flustered winds produce hurricanes over the sea and tornadoes over the land. Wakefulness in the middle of the night leads you to raid the fridge, and stubbing one's toe induces internal profanity in the person who never swears. Secondary causes like lit powder will force a bullet to fire across a battlefield, and a bullet once fired will cause a person to die. A secondary cause could be some wire crossed between my brain and the rest of my nervous system. Or that's the doctor's best guess—secondary causes. But there might not be one. My guess is as good as a doctor's, I suppose. "I'm being upstaged. / I thought I was writing this play."[2]

No, I wasn't. I never was. For the Playwright—the primary cause—is God. A sovereign, good God, who chose that I should be in pain right now. The reason? I don't know. It might be that one day I will stumble upon some grand lesson, that I'm limping my way toward a moral of the story I can only learn through physical pain. But realities are seldom that clear, certainly never that simple.

I don't know your story. I don't know which chapter, which page, which line God has thrust you into. Maybe angry flames of pain lick, relentless, through your body. Maybe fatigue weighs down every cell. Paralysis eats muscle, bones, and skin. Dystrophy dismantles muscle, fiber by fiber. Seizures slide through brains and scatter corrupted signals. Hallucinations haunt with too-vivid realities. Depression nods like an old friend.

Maybe the pain isn't in your body at all. Maybe it's in the hollow space where a marriage used to be—promises shattered, rings discarded along with your hopes and plans for the future. Maybe it's in the child who no longer calls. Perhaps you've felt friendships crumbling under the weight of betrayal, or a church dividing into wounds so deep they may never close. Maybe the job you built your life around vanished overnight. Maybe grief sits beside you at the dinner table where a loved one used to be.

Perhaps this doesn't feel like one of life's pages, but chapters and chapters—maybe even your whole story from beginning to end. Maybe God doesn't feel like the author—or you hope He isn't. For how could a good God have written this story for you?

I have lived all those questions from the inside. And suddenly, one day, the floodgates burst. I sat in bed with my Bible open on my lap and the pain shooting through my body and I just started crying and talking to God. It's strange the things that come to your mouth in moments like that.

As I prayed, sobbing and shaking, the words from a book whispered in the back of my mind: "Language went away and I prayed in a soft high-pitched lament any human listener would've termed a whine. We serve a patient God."[3]

It certainly was a whine then: "God, my body feels like it's breaking. God, I'm so sad—I don't understand what You're doing here. God, I feel like this is never going to end. God, I am scared. God, this is so heavy."

Over and over again: "God, help me! God, *please* help me!"

I poured out everything: all the pain, the fatigue, every aching bone, throbbing muscle, tingling nerve, and firing neuron. The heaviness, the weight, the darkness smothering me, the crushing burden of both pain and sadness in my chest. I laid it all before His throne—a broken, tearful, impoverished offering—a trash heap I had been hoarding far too long.

"Take it, Lord," I pleaded. My stomach twisted. I felt like I couldn't pray any harder. But I needed more words.

I scrambled through the pages of my Bible and started reading out loud, my voice weak and broken, barely above a whisper. Each line I stopped and prayed back to God: "Lord, You promise this. Lord, please do this. Lord, please help me to know this."

When I finished, I prayed some more, stumbling. I felt like a child learning to walk, chasing after her father, afraid she will be left behind. "Don't leave me here alone. I can't do this alone. Please. *Please.*"

I closed my Bible and felt stillness—not the stillness of peace or resolution, but the stillness that fills your heart when you have no tears left after a torrent of crying. In that moment, I had nothing left to give—no tears, no strength, no courage. And that was just where I needed to be.

You might have done everything you know how to do—pulled yourself together, held the pieces of your life in shaking hands, prayed until the words ran dry—yet you still feel like nothing has changed. You might have sat in bed, Bible open, tears soaking the pages, pain twisting through every part of you. The crying stopped, and nothing was left but the hollow stillness of being wrung dry.

For me, the pain hasn't left. The fight isn't over. But something has shifted. I'm not holding it alone anymore—I never was. I am tethered to the One who holds the story—even when I don't understand it.

You may not understand. You may even be furious at how your life is being written. You may feel like it's impossible to believe this pain could belong in the same story as goodness. But that's the invitation: not to understand, not to get stronger, but to stay. To stay in the story. To stay with the Author. Even if all you can do is whisper through gritted teeth, "I need You. Don't leave me. Please don't leave me."

That prayer reaches heaven. That prayer holds.

The Elephant of Pain

I had nightmares about my wedding day. In the weeks leading up to my wedding, I had dreams where I limped down the aisle and collapsed sometime before the "I dos." Humiliating—and the thought haunted me that if such a thing happened, it would be my fault, an artificial drama. Most people are unable to avoid some level of drama on their wedding day, but that would be drama to a horrifying degree. How many brides faint in their wedding dresses, or convulse in uncontrolled spasms on the floor? How many brides are carried out by the groom—not romantically, but medically, necessarily, frantically? Drama on such a grand scale seemed terrifying—and just the sort of thing of which this world is capable. Our world is infused with drama, in case you didn't know. Have you ever seen a butterfly?

None of that happened. Publicly. The only drama of the wedding day was beautiful, significant, and full of love. So was the wedding night, which included my husband carrying me downstairs and waiting up with me through the pain till the early hours of the morning. Neither of us slept. We had leftover tacos from Jack in the Box for breakfast. We reheated them by baking them in the oven to make them special. There are many ways to love each other.

I used to think my wedding vows would be the end of the fight—that our first kiss would close the chapter on my loneliness, my struggle, my pain. But our vows didn't end the struggle. They *anticipated* it. I carried mine right through the wedding day and straight into marriage. I dragged old life into new. And now—still—I am fighting. I am fighting a battle every moment of every day. My body is fighting to move, to act, to breathe. But my soul is fighting to live forever. Like the butterfly, I am caught in wind gusts, dancing toward a freedom that's always one draft away from disaster. On the days that lie most heavy, when my body lacks strength even to speak my thoughts out loud, I whisper and think prayers to the Lord. Some of the soul's greatest battles are fought from the isolated cage of a bed frame.

We don't like those kinds of battles. Butterfly battles. Flimsy wings, tossed in wind, calling attention to our visible fragility. No protecting the soft parts. The barely-making-it flight. There is beauty in that delicacy. But we would rather be strong. We don't like being upended by wind gusts, and we don't like the discomfort of other people knowing we are upended. We also don't like people *not* knowing.

"Are you in pain right now?" a family member asked after my diagnosis.

"I'm in pain every second," I replied.

"But . . . right *now*?"

"Yes."

She looked at me aghast. "A lot of pain?"

"Yes."

"I can stop talking if you want me to."

If you stopped talking whenever I'm in pain, you'd never talk to me again, I wanted to say. Instead, I smiled. "It's okay. It's not too bad right now. Besides," I added, seeing her concerned look, "I'm used to it."

She started talking again. "Um, okay . . . so anyway, I was just saying . . ." Her voice was light and forced; she faltered and giggled nervously. I tried to smile again, but the die was cast: It's uncomfortable to sit in the presence of pain—much less to chat, much less small talk. I knew she probably wished she had never asked. Everyone wants the progress report: *"I'm feeling better all the time." "This new medication seems to be helping." "The doctor has me on a treatment plan."*

But what if there is no progress? What if the answer is too honest? "I'm still hurting all the time." "My spouse left, and I don't think I'll ever trust love again." "My child still won't speak to me." "My faith is unraveling, and I don't know how to hold on to God anymore." "The people who were supposed to be my refuge are now my deepest source of pain." "I don't recognize my own life anymore, and I don't know how to keep going."

No one wants to hear that things are just the same—or worse—than the last time they asked you. Pain is the awkward elephant in the room. The conversation killer. There's no easy segue. No "anyway" is big enough. As I listened to that family member bump up against the elephant's massive legs, I thought maybe she had a point—I *was* having a hard time ignoring the pain. In fact, I had no idea what we were talking about. All my social energy had been spent on keeping a friendly face, smiling, nodding at the right moments, and sitting upright.

Pain raises the Awful Dilemma: Talk about your pain and make things awkward, or don't talk about your pain and feel awkward the whole time you're hiding it. Make people know, or make it so *nobody* knows. Go home and suffer in silence, or go out and let people in. I am hard-pressed between the two. I want to be indestructible, to barrel through as if nothing touches me. But I am fluttering, battered, wind-tossed—and it sometimes feels ridiculous to still be moving, still be alive, still be this fragile in a way I never intended.

Four Words That Take Everything

Jack in the Box will always remember us as the couple who came through their drive-through in a charcoal-gray suit and bridal gown, headband tiara still intact, wedding bouquet and veil in the back seat.

"Hi, can we have twenty tacos, please?"

"How many?"

"Twenty."

"Drive around to the window." The cashier's gaze flicked across us. "Did you all just get married?"

"Yep."

"Are you the ones that ordered twenty tacos?"

"Yes, that's us."

A long pause, through which I could hear her expression more than see it.

“Come drive around to the front.”

We drove around to the front and parked, waiting.

“You know,” said my husband, the new groom in his spotless suit, “we’re the kind of customers that cause arguments in the back over who gets to bring the food out.”

“That’s true. Even if no one else remembers today with us, the workers at Jack in the Box will.”

“We made their night.”

“Yeah, we did,” I replied, smoothing my white dress across my legs.

Ten minutes passed. One of the workers appeared at last, carrying the warm, greasy paper bag that contained our wedding dinner.

“Thank you for choosing Jack in the Box,” she said. “Also—congratulations.” There was a tickle of humor in her voice, as if she was in on a joke with us, a joke muted beneath fast-food-worker professionalism.

“Thank you,” my husband responded, muted beneath new-groom professionalism.

That twenty-one-year-old man I married is now my husband of four years. He is still good at playing the part. He doesn’t show it when my pain wears on him, when his conversation, wishes, or worries are shoved aside to prioritize taking care of me.

“I love you—don’t talk,” he says, holding me. My breathing is shallow, but he knows I’ll try to reply.

I give three gasps building up to it, and my body convulses, preparing: “I love you too,” I whisper.

I collapse back onto his chest, exhausted. My body continues shaking harder for several seconds, winding down from the fight. Those four words took it all out of me. Perhaps that’s how it’s supposed to be.

“You nut,” he says, and kisses me.

TWO

pieces

I first lost the ability to walk at the zoo. It was three weeks after we got married, and a week after the seizures and pain started to spread through my body. Only a few days before, I had been lying on the floor, convulsing, screaming in pain, begging Colton to take me to the emergency room. Maybe it seems strange that—with everything still unresolved—we decided to up and go to the zoo. The truth is, my faith in doctors was slipping. No one could determine what was wrong with me, and I craved distraction, the ability to *do* something.

Junction City, Kansas, doesn't have much to do, so the small zoo the next town over offered itself as a pleasing distraction. Or that is what I hoped. Instead, I spent the entire time angry. Angry at the struggle every step demanded, angry at Colton for making me stop and rest as my gait declined, angry at my body for rejecting the distraction I craved. Angry at the embarrassment of needing to rest between each exhibit, of sitting on a zoo bench alongside my husband and gripping a cane. Angry that my mind did not always have power over matter, for I strove as hard as my mind allowed, and my body only creaked vicious laughter in response.

We have a picture of us from that day, smiling up into the glare of the Kansas spring sun. Colton had tucked a small white flower into my unbrushed hair, which looks haphazardly playful, hanging at a horizontal angle over my ear. A stress-induced fever blister burns smack in the center of my upper lip, and my smile can't mask the exhaustion in my eyes.

On our way out, we went through the gift store. I counted down the seconds until I could drag myself to the parking lot without admitting defeat. A moment later, I couldn't walk, couldn't move, couldn't feel. From my hips downward, I stopped existing. Dragging yet weightless, my upper half floated above limbs that were a hundred miles below me, connected, yet unfelt.

I caught myself on one of the spinner racks next to me, then tried to motion to Colton without drawing attention to myself. Even at the moment of realizing I could no longer walk, I still feared someone would see me struggle.

It took a few moments to get Colton's attention. Once I did, I whispered hoarsely, "I can't move my legs." He put both arms around me and half carried, half dragged me out of the store, as I smiled weakly and murmured a "thanks" to the cashier behind the counter.

Colton got me over to the curb, and we sat down. "Take a moment," he said. "It will come back."

I lacked the strength to protest. We waited about ten minutes. My head still hung low, my chest hovering a few inches above my bent and useless legs.

"I want to try again—it won't get better than it is now," I said.

Colton nodded and supported my arm. "Help me as much as you're able. Try to connect to your legs again."

I swayed to my feet, my knees buckling underneath me. Colton's grip tightened on my upper arm and beneath my shoulder.

Then, at that moment of all moments—"Hey, guys! How are you?"

We looked up to see a couple from our Bible study smiling and coming toward us from across the hot black tarmac. We smiled back stiffly. Isn't it strange how you feel the urge to hide your pain the moment you need help the most? It feels like humility, but it's pride. You tell yourself, *I don't want to burden anyone with my problems*, but if you're honest, what you mean is, "I don't want to draw attention to my weakness or the fact that I *have* problems."

When someone sees me barely holding it together, I cover up, deflect, avoid revealing the mess I'm in, though it's that exact moment I could most use someone's help or compassion. There's something about being seen in a vulnerable state that feels unbearable. On that hot Kansas tarmac, I couldn't speak but wanted to hide my struggle behind a mask of small talk. Colton covered for me, got us through the social conventions, and hurried the conversation to a close. He began half carrying me to the car again the moment their backs were turned.

"Do you think they knew?" I whispered as we reached the car door.

"No. It's fine, babe," Colton said as he lowered me onto the seat.

We both knew the truth. We couldn't cover up the awkwardness of that scene. The next Bible study, Colton offered a vague explanation about my "health issues" and "leg weakness."

The husband gave a nervous chuckle. "Don't worry about it," he said. "You've only been married a couple weeks. I just thought you were being affectionate . . . you know, like newlyweds."

Colton laughed when he told me about it later. As odd as such a display of affection would've been at the zoo, it made more sense in the context of our newly married life than what had actually happened. At the time, however, embarrassment burned inside me—just one more reason to resent my failing body. I assumed losing the ability to walk marked the last thing that could reasonably be taken from me.

The next day, I woke up unable to speak.

I Am Ashamed

Suffering will either seal you forever in the grip of despair and anger or seal you deeper in the grasp of God. Suffering itself is not sin. Pain isn't punishment. Struggle isn't a consequence of some secret failing. But sin does *crouch at the door* of suffering, waiting to twist it open. Not usually through sudden rebellion or dramatic disbelief, but something much quieter—a subtle tinkering of the emotions, a vague "giving in just this once" to the indulgence of secret feelings that whisper untruths we don't fully believe.

Sin whispers, "Let yourself feel—just for this moment—that everything is a little unfair. Just *feel* that God is being unkind to you. You're not really *believing* that; you're just so tired . . . so disappointed . . . so aggrieved. It wouldn't be so hard except for the *timing* of it all. It's just one thing on top of another. You could bear it if only *this* were different."

But you should know what is happening. Sooner or later, your unguarded feelings shape untrue thoughts—thoughts about God, the way you perceive Him—not because your doctrine has changed, but because you just "feel" differently about Him. This is why Isaiah warns, "Woe to him who strives with him who formed him, a pot among earthen pots! Does the clay say to him who forms it, 'What are you making?' or 'Your work has no handles'?" (Isaiah 45:9 ESV).

I often feel like a pot without handles. Clumsy, useless, awkward—the one in the kitchen that no one takes off the shelf. "God, I could do so much more for You if You hadn't given me this *exhaustion* that weighs on every cell, these *seizures* that sap my mind and strength, this *pain* that steals my focus—all these extra obstacles between me and doing the right thing. God, I would be so much more *useful* if You had made me with handles!" I mask my resentment under a guise of suffocated holiness.

My feelings are the god I worship in a field of outcast prayers. Isaiah 45:11–12 provides God's answer to me: "Will you command me concerning my children and the work of my hands? I made the earth and created man on it; it was my hands that stretched out the heavens, and I commanded all their host" (ESV).

If you are confused, wondering what on earth God is doing with you, asking, "Why this, Lord? And why me?" then you are in good company. You ask alongside Abraham and Moses, the whole nation of Israel, the psalmists, the prophets, the judges, the exiles, the disciples, and the church. You are alongside a cloud of witnesses who also wondered and asked God, "Why?" God didn't always tell them the answer—in fact, He usually didn't. He told them to obey and trust Him, walking forward into the unknown in faith. God promises to use all His pots well. Even—especially—when they're handle-less.

One night, I cried and struggled in terror as I saw someone I loved trying to kill me. Colton didn't know—couldn't possibly know—what I was seeing on the dark edge of our living room wall. When I started to stagger at the kitchen sink, he held me up and pulled me into the room where I could lie down on the floor. I fought against him as he pulled me in there. He lowered me onto the ground and I struggled harder, barely feeling the flood of tears on my cheeks, the crack in my cries. I screamed, feeling the exposure, the vulnerability of being laid on my back in that awful place.

"Please don't hurt me—please don't hurt me!"

"Darling, no. Sydney . . . Sydney, I would never hurt you. Please, no . . . please, baby."

He bent over me, his arms around me, his head against my chest, the weight of his legs curled around the sides of my waist.

I heard the pain in his voice. I knew somehow, I had caused it. Fresh guilt and terror and confusion surged into my chest.

"I'm sorry, I'm sorry," I sobbed to his shadow. Then, "I'm sorry, I'm sorry," and I spoke to the shape behind him, the shape that was clearer than everything else, my brother lying on the floor, and *them*, a monstrous visage, crumpled with grief and wild with pain, coming for me.

"Get off! Get off! Don't touch me!" I screamed, flailing my arms wildly against Colton's chest.

I saw his shape retreat against the door, distant and blurry, the red of his shirt the brightest part of him. I rolled over and sobbed into the carpet and convulsed for a long time. Then, my mind went blank. No terror anymore, only heavy, weight-filled exhaustion. I lay still, feeling my own breathing, the threads of the carpet against my face, the weight of my chest across my arms, the wetness on my cheeks. I opened my eyes. Colton sat against the door, staring at me, clear and real. His red shirt, quite close. I saw his face. He told me later the episode lasted just shy of two hours. I slept most of the next day, exhausted.

I had episodes like this—every night—when my mind forsook me, moments of total fear and confusion, seeing and hearing things that weren't there, speaking and thinking as a frightened child.

Waking up always felt like realizing I had dragged someone else into my own nightmare, except he knew I was dreaming, but I did not. I stood literally helpless, vulnerable, naked before my husband. But rather than see my shame, Colton held me, comforted me, loved me, helped me, protected me, served me. He listened to my confused fears and childish questions and explained things to me again and again. He held me when I fought and screamed against him; he undressed me, washed me, and clothed me again. I saw shame, brokenness, exposure. Colton saw the woman he loved.

That is what Isaiah promises. He is saying, "You feel like you cry out to God and He doesn't hear you! You think this is all in vain! You think you are a useless lump of clay! You live in fear and confusion and pain! But God hears you. God knows. And God promises you will not be ashamed and confused forever. He is forming you for something beautiful and glorious. He looks at you and sees His beautiful bride, whom He loves. He will hold you, protect you, comfort you, love you, clothe you. You say you are Broken, but God calls you Beloved."

Shame is here, lingering in unspoken corners. The way you shrink into yourself when you need help. The way you smile and hurry through small talk rather than letting someone see your weakness. The way you tell yourself, *This isn't my fault*, while still feeling the crushing burden of failure. The shame of needing help when you used to be independent. The shame of a diagnosis people don't understand. The shame of not being able to hold everything together the way you once could.

Shame and guilt are different. Guilt is objective: a true conviction that follows sin or wrongdoing. But shame can creep in even when you've done nothing wrong. It whispers, "You are not enough. You are a burden. You are broken. This is your fault." It convinces you that needing help is the same thing as failing, that being seen in your weakness is something to fear.

I try to hide it. I want to carry my suffering quietly, gracefully. But deep down, I fear what people would think if they really saw me—if they saw the way my body betrays me at my most vulnerable moments, the way I sometimes still crumble under the weight of it all.

We cry out, feeling we have sought the Lord in vain. But God responds, "I am the Lord, and there is no other. I did not speak in secret, in a land of darkness; *I did not say to the offspring of Jacob, 'Seek me in vain'*" (Isaiah 45:18–19 ESV, emphasis added). Don't try to hide your shame from God—He already knows. Hold it up to Him with open hands. Show Him. Tell Him why. Cry to Him. Ask Him to take your shame from your heart, to help you trust Him even when your body cries against trust. Ask Him to deliver you. Tell Him of your weariness, your burden, your heavy-laden soul. Ask Him for rest. Coming to the Lord with your shame, your anger, your confusion, your grief, and your pain is not sin—it is faith.

I Am Broken

I couldn't open my eyes. I tried, but they rolled back, my lids falling, fluttering, dropping again. I kept peeking to check if I could still see. Light flashed, blurred images, unfocused. I could see, but I was blind. Seeing without seeing. Colton spoke to me, touched my hand, but his voice came from far away, and I couldn't make out the words. He squeezed my fingers, and I squeezed back, delayed, several seconds later. The Translators—whatever tiny nerves and signals communicate between brain and fingers—were asleep on the job.

To tear down the altar to my own self-pity, I decided to name different parts of my body. It really wasn't much of an imagination stretch—they already felt like someone else. My right leg I called Karl. He was named after this guy I knew from my work. Whenever Karl slacked off, I got saddled with a bunch of extra stuff to do. I always wanted the opportunity to give Karl a piece of my mind, so now I gave myself the luxury of saying things like: "Karl, you suck at your job." "Karl, how am I supposed to do my own thing when I have to do the work for both of us?" "Karl, you need to get your life together"—and other delicious tidbits.

I called my left leg Jacob. Jacob is a homebody, pretty selfish and lazy at times. He tries to take what he can without giving back. Jacob in the Bible also walked with a limp, which seemed fitting. My husband reminded me that an *angel* wounded Jacob, but being that I didn't have a solid diagnosis yet, I thought it too early to exclude this possibility for my case as well.

My ability to speak I named Friday. And since my speech was called Friday, my mind had to be Crusoe—trying to salvage all the pieces he could, bind them together, make what use of them he may. Crusoe and Friday both knew all the right words and had no way to say them to each other. Educated minds with the language of cavemen.

Crusoe was always trying to get Friday to understand. Trying to get Friday to repeat the words after him.

Brokenness is the loss of something whole—the redefinition of oneself when the pieces scatter. The moment you realize your body is no longer a seamless extension of your will, but a collection of failing dramatists, one F away from dropping out. The work of searching for yourself in the ruins, salvaging what you can, naming what you cannot fix, and learning to live with the remains.

If I believed brokenness was beautiful—*wonderful*—all by itself, I'd be something in between an asylum-destined Pollyanna and a certifiable psychopath. But Christian brokenness doesn't just stand in the rubble; it also looks for redemption. My hope isn't in the fact that one day all my pieces will lead me onward to something great and complete, but in how my future redemption in Christ will work *backward* to unravel all that is broken and incomplete now—to make these pieces beautiful. To rename my body—not Karl and Jacob and Friday—but Sydney as she was created to be. Sydney Redeemed.

I Am Waiting

Each day felt like waking up in the body of a person with a different disability. Here is a taste of the mute and the stutterer. Here is a glimpse of the paralyzed and the lame. This is what epilepsy feels like. Here is a shadow of the life of an invalid. Here is pain, of which many people drink deeply without a moment to catch their breath. Here is a touch of insanity and confusion. Here is a new disease every day.

Disability had always felt strange and foreign to me. The lives—and bodies—of those physically suffering were something I could not understand or feel comfortable near. Now, I realized—as I stuttered, fumbled, fell, hallucinated, screamed, and staggered with my unbalanced, distorted gait—that disability no longer felt foreign but intensely and strenuously human.

What had once been a vague but naive compassion for those who struggled now surged as a deep and tear-filled empathy and awe. "May I sit at your table, please?" I felt like saying. "I am new here and don't know much, but I think some of us are hurting in the same ways, and I feel so alone. I'm not sure if I'm 'disabled enough' to sit at this table, but let me at least sit at your feet. My suffering is so small compared to that of others, but it feels overwhelming to me."

My disability changes every day. I lose the same things over and over. But I also get to switch things up—rest in the privilege of unpredictability, the predictability of steady loss, the surprise of cycled recovery. Unpredictability makes history. All the best stories count on it: the unexpected. The chaotic descent, deeper and deeper, through the twists and turns to the lowest level. Only a fool closes the covers when the story looks bleak. He knows it doesn't end there. Sam and Frodo don't stay on the mountain. Jim doesn't remain locked in the shed. Crusoe figures out how to leave the island. Jean Valjean is redeemed. Christ does not stay in the tomb.

Tomorrow, I ask, what will happen? Perhaps great eagles, or ropes in pie, foreign ships, an acquitted thief, the return of God, a man raised from the dead.

Or perhaps the question one more time: "Do you love me?"

"Yes, Lord," we say. "You know. You know."

THREE

laughter

Only my fingers moved, jerking involuntarily at times, tight and stiff, a little too warm, tiny splinters of pain reminding me that even writing is physical work. Were I an old man before the rain, I might've given out a contented moan, rubbed my knees, stretched my shoulders, and grunted something like, "Oh, my bones weren't made to live this long."

But I was not an old man. I was twenty-two, and it was two in the morning, the hour of the sad, the lonely, the insomniac. Maybe you know this hour too. Maybe you've also lain awake watching the ceiling in the dark, wondering how the next day will ask more of you than you have to give. Maybe your pain isn't physical—grief or fear, regret or depression, a mind or heart that is weary of struggling. *I don't want to waste my pain*—that sentence stings a little even to write. It might sound like I'm saying pain is good, or that we should grin and bear it. It might sound like I'm saying every agony has a seen purpose—silver linings to dreaded clouds, which you will only see if you dare to look hard enough. No. Pain is awful. It was never meant to exist in God's good world. It is so awful, the Son of God came to this earth in broken human flesh and gave His life to defeat it.

Yet, since pain is here right now, and we with it, I don't want it to be for nothing. I don't want it to hook me from the inside out and turn me into a numb, bitter, hollow-eyed navel-gazer, entombed in despair. I want it—somehow—to be gathered up by God and reshaped into redemption. I know He will do it. He promises. But at two in the morning, it is too easy—too easy to become jaded and consumed by discouragement, by the permanency of struggle, by the stretching forth of future years that might bring no change, or bring change for the worse.

Insomnia has long been my bosom enemy. Anxiety introduced us. Depression drew us closer. Maybe you know her too; she's visited you—stretched herself out beside you in the dark, unwelcome but familiar, sharing your mattress. Many nights, she brings her friends Nightmares and Flashbacks along for kicks and giggles, for when things get boring and she can see us drifting a bit. "None of that," she says, rising dark and phantomlike above our heads. "Have a shot of terror." I imagine her cracking her knuckles, but they never make a sound.

I thought Insomnia had left me for a while, moved away, or finally decided to get a life. Then I met Pain accidentally. I don't remember how we met, but Insomnia was with her. They're with me now, side by side, an unsplittable duo.

The kindhearted and innocent say I should dump this toxic group.

"Take a deep breath. It's because you're too anxious all the time!"

"I know someone who healed herself by going on keto."

"Don't speak that over yourself."

"Stay positive. I know you'll get better!"

People say those kinds of things enough times, and eventually you'll just smile. Those people mean well. But you survived the hazing, and they don't know what you're in for.

But I have another enemy, one I often forget because she lies in the shadows. Apathy is here too. Cloaked in subtlety, in quietude, in one plodding moment followed by the next. Pain gave her the key to enter. Pain is the excuse to let her reign. She is the mistress that promises in reverse: Instead of promising to give much, she promises to only take a little—and then takes all in the end.

When I say I don't want to waste my pain, I mean I don't want to surrender to Apathy. She is a thief, creeping in through the window when the suffering lingers too long, when the answers don't come, when the weight of it all presses down so heavily I wonder if I should stop fighting. Apathy is not rest; she is a surrender to meaninglessness. And that is the last thing pain should be.

In the fight against her, there is a real, practical demand for physical tasks and labor. For getting up and accomplishing what you can with your moments and energy. For blessing others in the ways you are able. But there are days, perhaps years, perhaps a lifetime, from which illness can rob this physical ability. It is far easier now for Apathy to win—when you fall into the trap of thinking the value and meaning of your suffering is found only in what you accomplish and produce through it—or in overcoming it. Apathy crouches at the nightstand beside your bed and whispers: "Your suffering is meaningless." When it's dark, and there's no other distraction, it is easy to listen.

But it is a lie.

Apathy tells you your suffering is meaningless. But God wastes nothing. Even pain.

This fight, this race, this devotion to *not wasting your pain* does not come from physical exertion, or accomplishments, or money, or the number of lives you have changed. It isn't a fight to hold on to your strength, or energy, or pre-illness capacity and stamina. Those things will slip through your hands like water no matter how tightly you try to hold them. This fight—this fight to not waste your pain—is a fight against unbelief. A fight to trust that God has not abandoned you here. A fight to rest when every struggling, screaming, self-sabotaging instinct inside you says, "Do something. Fix it. Prove yourself. Earn your way out."

Some people are called to pain the way others are called to abundance. Or maybe we all, like Job, are called to both. Risk of loss is the price of blessing. One has never existed without the other, even in Eden. The race is won by collapsing into His mercy. Even the most broken sinner may do that. *Only* the most broken sinner can.

Apathy's Lie

Perhaps this all seems like a bit much right now. If there is meaning in our suffering, why does it feel so meaningless? If God is in control, why does He let it continue? And if He isn't, why pray to Him at all? The first time I wrestled with these questions was when my little brother, Isaiah, lay in a hospital bed at ten years old, a spiderweb of tubes and wires across his face and body. Machines breathed for him while thousands of Christians around the world prayed for God to heal. God did not heal. At least not in the way *I wanted*. Isaiah took his last breath on this earth and his first breath in glory. Amid the initial shock and grief came a transcendent strength and courage—a peace that settled over the hospital room like a heavy but sacred weight. But in the months that followed, when the grief became more real and painful, prayer started to feel meaningless.

Maybe you've been there too—standing in the wreckage of suffering, staring at God with your hands in fists, unsure if you even want to talk to Him. My prayers in those months were tangled and bitter. *God, comfort me in the pain You have caused. (Though I think it would be easier if You hadn't caused it at all.) Lord, help me survive this. (Though I don't know why I think this will work when so many Christians prayed the same for Isaiah and You said no.) Lord, I want to feel Your presence in this. (But also, I'm angry, so I would appreciate some space.)*

Maybe you've had your own versions of this prayer, the kind that feels like flinging words into the void, that barely makes it past your lips before resentment and exhaustion swallow it whole. Maybe you've even subtly whispered your own terms to God, as I did, that this must be the only breaking point, the moment when the suffering is capped, the end of what a person can take. *God, just so You know, You've reached the quota on reasonable suffering. Only one great undoing per lifetime is allowed. I understand You will work good through this, but no further suffering will be appreciated. The statute of limitations lasts the rest of my miserable life.*

When our suffering lingers, when the pain does not resolve, when the prayers seem unanswered, it is here, in this aching in-between, that the fight against unbelief is most needed. The full healing of all God's people and their every affliction awaits the second coming of Christ. But the end of our hope is not just the redemption of our bodies but the glorifying of our souls. Our suffering in this world is directly preparing for us an eternal weight of glory that cannot be compared to our present affliction (2 Corinthians 4:16–18).

Many of Jesus' miracles vanquished bodily pain. But He did not stop there. Jesus promised more than a healed body. When we glimpse future restoration—whether through moments of physical relief, medical interventions, or the inexplicable peace that surpasses understanding—we glimpse the truth that our suffering will not have the final word. Even Jesus' healing miracles on this earth, as wondrous as they were, were not the ultimate goal. They pointed beyond themselves to the Healer of Souls, to the One who will, in the end, wipe away every tear and make all things new. This means that when we do not receive healing now, we are not abandoned. Even when pain remains, it is not meaningless. Every moment of endurance, every act of trust in the darkness, every cry of dependence on Him is shaping us for eternity. Our broken bodies and weary spirits testify to a deeper reality: This world is not our home, and our hope is not in temporary relief, but in the full redemption to come.

Tears and Oil

I saw a glimpse of that redemption in the small, shabby living room of our first home—an apartment complex inappropriately named Grandview Plaza. The hollow staircase echoed with soldiers' boots through paper-thin, pilled carpet at all hours of the night. Where people looked at you a little sideways, eyes squinting in the Kansas heat. Where arguments, fights—even crimes—rolled through the units with the resigned jadedness of the ordinary.

Back when Colton and I were dating long-distance, I soon learned our phone call would come extra late on Wednesdays—Bible study night. He'd call hours afterward, buzzing with stories of laughter, deep conversation, and the highly caffeinated coffee from the Ingallses' home espresso machine—a component every Fort Riley soldier saw as a profound extension of the Ingalls family ministry.

The first Wednesday after our honeymoon, Colton took me to Bible study half an hour early out of sheer excitement—beaming with all the tenderness and pride that befits a new husband. He led me around by the hand, introducing me to everyone by name: "Larry, this is *Sydney*," as if the name carried an inside meaning everyone but me was aware of. I beamed at his side, smiling, shy, and extremely gratified.

Bible study was the first place we shared what was happening to me. People asked for updates. They prayed. They watched as Colton half carried me out of the room a dozen times to lay me down on the couch and help me recover.

One Saturday afternoon, Colton walked into our bedroom, phone in hand.

"Larry wants to know if the group can come pray for you," he said, grinning a little. "They also want to . . . um . . . anoint your head with oil."

"They *what*?"

"From James. You know, 'pray over the sick . . . anoint them with oil.' But you don't have to say yes to the oil part," he added, still grinning. "Larry asked, and I kinda guessed you wouldn't want that bit."

I glanced around our apartment—piles of unpacked boxes, Army gear strewn across the floor, a spare tire propped against the wall, and one solitary green-blue, faux-leather love seat that had seen better days—the only actual sitting place in the whole living room. I hadn't showered, and I was still in the same wrinkled dress and gray sweatshirt I'd thrown on two days earlier.

Colton caught the look. "Babe. Seriously. They're coming because you're sick. A clean apartment would actually be weird right now."

I sighed. "Okay . . . yes to the prayer. And, um . . . no to the oil."

"Got it."

I hesitated. "Also, do I . . . do I look *really bad* right now?"

Colton kissed the top of my frizzy hair. "You always look beautiful," he said.

I pulled away, squinting up at him. "No, really. Be honest."

He stepped back, scrutinizing me up and down. "You look beautiful," he offered again. "You just don't look . . . well."

My face fell.

"But that's fine!" he said, pulling me close. "They're literally coming over because you're *not* well! They don't expect you to look . . . I don't know . . . *great* right now."

An hour later, six people piled onto the unvacuumed floor of our living room. I curled up next to Colton on the love seat, his arm around me, his fingers stroking my hair—getting snagged every few inches in tangles, which he gallantly pretended not to notice.

One by one, they prayed. It was the first time I ever saw Colton cry. In the five years of knowing each other before I got sick, including our wedding day, I never saw him shed a single tear—but this prayer broke him. His head dropped into his hands. His shoulders shook. "God, please heal her because . . . *I don't know what to do!*"

I sagged against him and stroked his chest. There was no pretending that day. Not for him. Not for me. In this burst of vulnerability, his brokenness stood over mine—not as my savior, or my nurse, or even my invincible pillar of protection, but as my husband. A man who loved me. Who didn't have the answers. Who wondered, and struggled, and wept beside me on the blue-green couch in front of our friends. Who brought his own breaking to the feet of Jesus, right alongside mine.

When the prayer ended and everyone filed out, Colton helped me back to bed, kissed my lips, and pulled the sheet around me. The pain didn't leave. The fatigue didn't lift. The brief social interaction had taken everything out of me. But the aroma of prayer and my husband's tears still lingered in our living room along thin, white drywall, seeping into the blue-green love seat, circling the spare tire in the corner. I may not receive healing in this life, and whether I receive healing or not, my body will suffer, break, change, and torment me before the end. But when healing feels far away, when my suffering stretches on without end, I remember this: Christ has come, and He will come again. Every moment of perseverance is a step toward that day.

Pray for healing, yes, but pray for more than healing: "Lest I should be exalted above measure by the abundance of the revelations, a thorn in the flesh was given to me, a messenger of Satan to buffet me" (2 Corinthians 12:7).

Pray this suffering leads to holiness. Pray God uses the battle of your body to win the greater battle in your soul: "Concerning this thing I pleaded with the Lord three times that it might depart from me" (verse 8).

Pray He would not only heal your flesh but also heal your heart: "He said to me, 'My grace is sufficient for you, for My strength is made perfect in weakness'" (verse 9).

In the day of His coming, the healing will not just be of your body but of all things—your sorrow, your emptiness, your disappointments, even the wounds you cannot see: "Therefore most gladly I will rather boast in my infirmities, that the power of Christ may rest upon me . . . For when I am weak, then I am strong" (verses 9–10).

Hold fast, for He is not wasting a single drop of your pain.

The God in the Mirror

Colton and I lounged across the sheets of our bed, trying to avoid the Kansas heat, eating ice cream out of coffee mugs. It was a few weeks after our wedding, and I decided to confide an embarrassing wedding fear I'd had to him.

"You wanna know something dumb?" I said, trying to sound casual but feeling vulnerable to the bone. "Before the wedding, I had this tiny, secret fear that I'd be too heavy to do our send-off! Like, you wouldn't be able to lift me or something."

Colton paused mid-spoonful and gave me the look of a man who's just been told his truck can't pull a trailer. "You didn't think I could lift you?"

I saw my new-wife blunder. "No, of course I knew *you* could lift me," I stammered. "I didn't mean that you—couldn't. I just worried *I* was too heavy—not for you—just like, a me thing. Like, too heavy as a person . . ."

As someone who was playing mental catch-up after years of disordered eating, something still whispered to me when I looked in the mirror: "You're too big."

Colton and I had planned our send-off for the wedding—he

would pick me up and carry me out under the flower petals and cheers of our immediate family. But sometimes when I looked in the mirror I had been petrified at the thought: *What if I'm too heavy? What if he can't lift me? What if I embarrass both of us on our wedding day?*

Colton's open mouth told me I wasn't making this any better. Without a word, he set down his mug of ice cream, picked me up, slung me over his shoulder, and started dropping squats.

"*Do ya still think that?*" he shouted, heaving my body up and down as if I were a crocheted doily around his neck.

"No," I gasped, laughing and embarrassed. "I do not still think that."

He set me back down, and I staggered dizzily against the bed. "Too heavy for me to lift," he muttered, offended, under his breath. Then he retrieved his mug and took a bite of ice cream. "What sort of *nonsense* . . ."

The problem, of course, wasn't that I thought my husband wasn't strong. It's that I wasn't thinking about him at all. Even my perceived concern in his direction was obsession over myself. The mirror shrank my whole world down to me. *Too big, too much, too embarrassing* somehow collided in my mind with *too small, too weak, not enough.* And it only took seeing him again—his real strength, his real love—to make all those fears look ridiculous in hindsight. The real Colton dashed all my worries away.

That's what pain does to us. It distorts the mirror. We look at the weight of it and think: *This is too much. Too heavy. Too big. Even for God to carry.*

But nothing is too heavy for God.

Right now, the pain may feel random, like a senseless dice roll, a cosmic gamble on your life and happiness. But Scripture reminds us: "The lot is cast into the lap, but its every decision is from the LORD" (Proverbs 16:33). A human-level dice roll is a God-level order of love. A human-level chapter of pain is a God-level storybook of glory. Human-level pointlessness is God-level purpose. Human-level insanity is God-level salvation.

If you, like me, are struggling to believe that right now, if the only prayer you can manage is, "God, help me see even a glimpse of meaning in this," then take heart—He hears you. He is the Author, and He is writing a story so beautiful that when you see it in full, you will read it forever. So great is our suffering that only the God who ordained it can strengthen us to endure. If your suffering plumbs you to a depth you cannot fathom, then you need a God with unfathomable goodness, love, and purpose to sustain you through it. If your whole life feels like stumbling through a language you can't understand, you need the Great Interpreter who knows the story better than you do.

If I know God is the One who has brought this pain to me, then I know He is the One who can deliver me from it. If I know God ordained these trials, I know He will strengthen me to bear them. If I know God brought this hurt to me, I know He will not allow it to harm me. If He has brought desolation, I know He will not let it destroy me. If He promises an end, I know He will give me endurance to that end—and that it will be a good end.

This is why the sovereignty of God has become so precious to me and to so many who suffer. It means not a single ounce of our pain is wasted. None of it happens because God is weak, or cruel, or careless. The same power and wisdom that govern our suffering right now is the same power that promises to one day deliver us from it.

The Last Laugh

I sagged over the kitchen counter, trying to think. The coffee scoop was still in my hands, which trembled and tingled with uncontrolled tremors and nerve endings of pain. *Wait . . . did I say one or two? How many scoops do I usually do? Is it three? Am I on three?* The scoop felt like a nine-pound hammer between my thumb and forefinger. I squinted at the blurry buttons on the coffee machine, my brain stalling out.

I dropped my head onto my arms, overwhelmed by the idea of finishing this task. For a long time, I leaned there, my head buzzing with static, neurons misfiring, eyes straining to make out the glowing numbers on the coffee maker: 7:52. *I have no backup plan for this,* I thought. *I don't know how to make coffee.*

At times the sovereignty of God is a soft pillow for my weary head. But other times it seems like a distant doctrine, something people express belief in—*God is in control*—when they don't know what else to say. Yes, He is, but what does that mean for the person who can't even count coffee scoops?

A few weeks after my neurological symptoms started, I decided to bake cookies. I had been a wife for about a month at this point, and my dreams of creating a beautiful, tidy home and serving homemade meals every night had gone down the drain. But this one day, while Colton was at work, I felt a rare flicker of energy. I wanted to use it well. I would make cookies. That's what good wives do. At least, I had heard something to that effect.

I scoured our scant pantry for some ingredients and selected a simple recipe that involved mostly flour, butter, and brown sugar. That seemed pretty foolproof.

I shuffled around the kitchen using a broomstick as a cane and started dumping ingredients into a bowl, measuring, stirring, leaning on the counter when the work got to be too much. When the preheated oven beeped, I looked for a cookie sheet. In the oven drawer, in each cabinet. Pantry. Dishwasher. Nothing.

Panic surged. All this work, all this staggering around, all this lifting and pouring, dough mixing, preparing to fill the house with good-wife aromas—had it all been for *nothing*? I stood a moment, feet planted for balance, broomstick in hand, and stared hard at the hot and empty oven. No. I had been through worse. This would not break me.

I scanned our cabinets again and found a nine-by-thirteen glass Pyrex baking dish. This would work, right? How different could it really be from a metal cookie sheet? I rolled the dough into picturesque balls, spaced them at the bottom of the glass Pyrex, and put the whole thing in the oven. This world holds a lot of happiness, like a body that cannot contain a laugh. And people in this world aren't supposed to feel like they're dying. I shut the oven door.

Twenty-five minutes later, I opened the door to my masterpiece and my stomach dropped. There were no cookies. Just one lumpy, amorphous mess—something between a failed cake and the formless deep of Genesis 1:2. Determined to salvage this somehow, I took a spatula and hovered over the formless void, trying to cut it into cookie shapes, but they simply crumbled. I pulled out the Pyrex and stared at it, defeated. Colton would be home in thirty minutes. There was a mess in the kitchen, flour in my unwashed hair, and now I had nothing to show for it. We were broke and I had wasted ingredients, not to mention my precious energy, which I could have used on other, more useful things, like *showering.*

I stared at the Pyrex, head cocked to one side, eyes squinted. *Please, let me find a way to salvage this,* I prayed. *What can I turn this into?* Not cookies . . . no . . . it was closer to cake than cookies. But no shape. Just crumbs. Crumbs. Like cake crumbs.

Oh my word, crumb cake!

I had heard of crumb cake before—on Pinterest and in books—so it was definitely a real thing. I wasn't sure what crumb cake looked like, but then again, I was pretty sure Colton didn't know either. And, judging by the name, it couldn't look *that* different from the mess that was on my stovetop. I took the spatula again with renewed energy and carefully spread the nebulous mass, making it flat and even, pressing the crumbs together into a firmer, tighter cake shape. I stood back and admired my work. It wasn't *terrible*. The flattened cookie looked like it still tasted good. It still smelled delicious. *What do men know about cakes anyway?* I thought. I was pretty sure Colton would trust my expertise.

Colton came home to a smiling wife in a good-smelling kitchen. The door swung open and stayed there. His Army bag thumped to the floor, and his boots treaded across the yellow tile in a heartbeat. Planting a kiss on my hair, he looked at me, smiling.

"What is that *amazing* smell?" he asked.

I beamed and gestured to the stove. "I made you a crumb cake!" I said, full of smiles and profound dignity. He looked at the cake, and looked at me, then back at the cake. His smile deepened, and he pulled me into a hug, kissed me, and whispered with all the tender sincerity of a romantic man, "I love when you make me cakes that don't exist."

I pulled back. "It does exist!" I stammered. "It's—it's a *crumb cake*! It's on *Pinterest*!"

He winked. "Oh, I know. I love crumb cake."

I pulled out of his arms and looked again at the cake I'd cobbled together on the stovetop. As I stood next to Colton, the cake no longer looked like a Pinterest miracle. It looked exactly like what it was: a smashed-together, lumpy pile of crumbs.

Then I felt Colton's arms around me. He was laughing. *Hard.* Laughing with me. Laughing because he knew exactly what I had tried to do.

"I love you!" he said, spinning me around. "Thank you for my crumb cake!"

And suddenly, I was laughing too. Broomstick down, we hugged in the kitchen in front of that good-smelling pile of crumbs. We ate it straight out of the Pyrex with spoons. It was gone in two days. To this day, Colton will remind me with tender, loving eyes of the crumb cake I once baked for him.

Sometimes, however, I feel for certain that I am the one being laughed *at*. With a shaking fist, I hand the microphone over to Pain and Insomnia. They hold it to their lips and breathe out long and slow: "Have a shot of terror."

I didn't know Depression had joined us.

She nods, familiar.

And so I pray for laughter.

Not because I see the meaning in all this yet. Not because I feel better. Not because I understand. But because I know—however distant it feels right now—that God does not waste a single drop of pain. That all His promises hold firm and true. That He is deeper than Depression, more vigilant than Anxiety, more wakeful than Insomnia, more present than Pain, more steadfast than Apathy.

That one day, whether in this life or the next, I will see the joke played upon death. That because of Christ we will have the last laugh. That though sorrow burrows deep, joy will dig deeper still. And when I pray for laughter, I don't pray into the void. One day, these truths will feel as real and comforting to me as they truly are.

I serve a God who works in messes. He feeds five thousand people with five loaves of crumbs. He reshapes brokenness into masterpieces, sorrow into seeds of joy.

He invites us to a wedding. I think there will be cake.

FOUR

carried

The ER doctor snapped the second time I came in, paralysis spreading through my body like pain, like death. "You have a rapidly degenerating brain condition!" he said. "Find a doctor who can do real testing, and stop coming back here." He glared at me. "Find a doctor, or you could die. Whatever this is will likely kill you."

I had spent five hours staring at the spots that swelled and swirled across the ceiling, too weak to care I was hallucinating again. Five hours unable to move, in excruciating pain. Colton waited in the ER parking lot, banned by COVID-19 regulations before I even got into a room. I was alone, placid, without feeling, as I received the news from the doctor. The fact that I might be dying elicited no surprise. It seemed obvious. I could feel death creeping through me every day.

The hospital staff let me call Colton to come get me, but he couldn't come inside. He met me just outside the entrance and wheeled me to the car. I'd been dismissed, still in pain, still unable to move. Three days earlier I'd also been seen after my hands became paralyzed while driving back from a date night at a burger joint. That was the first symptom I had recognized as neurological. More had occurred every day since.

"What did the doctor say?" Colton's words snapped me back to the present.

I noticed he had unwrapped the comforter we'd just bought. I sat quiet, staring at the plastic packaging strewn across the seats. The March morning bristled with cold, and he couldn't run the heat for five hours in the car while he waited for me. A strange, disjointed gratitude filled me that I hadn't brought that blanket inside our home yet.

I told him without feeling. Without surprise. Colton stared ahead through our cracked car windshield, his hand on my hand. I looked at him, and my stomach twisted. *I want a whole life with him . . . but I don't want a whole life of this.*

I'd struggled with depression before I became sick. I longed for heaven, for peace, for an end to pain, for *home*. I don't think it's a sin to long for heaven. It's a design feature, not a flaw. The more we become immersed in the sorrows and sufferings of life in this broken world, the more natural, beautiful, and concentrated is our longing to be with Christ in glory. The pain and exhaustion weighed down and tingled every cell, but beneath it all, excitement glimmered: *I might be going to heaven soon.*

But then I would think of Colton, and my heart would tear in two. I wanted to be in heaven, to be glorified, beautiful, whole, perfect, complete, to see the saints and loved ones gone before me—to see my little brother Isaiah—to find an end to the suffering that seemed such a heavy part of my life on this earth. But I found it hard that all this should come right at the point in my life I expected to be happiest. That heaven should come after honeymoon—that the comfort, intimacy, and protection of my earthly husband should be cast off so suddenly for my heavenly One. I thought of the future I might be leaving early—a lifetime of marriage with this man whom I loved, future children—and felt my heart might break.

I had often felt the raw honesty of Paul's confession in Philippians 1:23: "My desire is to depart and be with Christ, for that is far better." Now I felt the agony of his quandary: "Yet which I shall choose I cannot tell. I am hard pressed between the two" (verses 22–23 ESV).

Of course, I didn't have that choice. Life or death would be chosen for me. *My desire is to depart and be with Christ, for that is far better.* Yes, better than marriage, better than children, better than years of earthly life. Those things were wonderful, but not wonderful like glory. They were things I had dreamed of and hoped for in a *healthy* body, not a disabled one. My dream future had been bright-eyed and bushy-tailed, not broken and full of pain.

My future didn't diverge—as I imagined it would—between happiness on earth and happiness in heaven, but between unending pain on earth and relief in heaven. God forbade me to choose death myself, but perhaps He had chosen it for me. To die wouldn't mean losing a future of fulfillment but a future of brokenness. I wouldn't be quitting a blissful happily-ever-after but a difficult struggle. I would not be relinquishing my dream of future children but the cold iron of this purposeless cage. I would be setting aside not my dream but my nightmare. Yet, I mourned the loss of the dream. I mourned the future that would never happen. I longed for heaven, and the longing itself felt like a robbery. God exposed the longing by stripping the rest away; the longing was carved into the cavern of my loss. The more I thirsted for heaven's relief, the more I knew my own parchedness, my erosion, my despair. The deeper the river flowed, deeper still ran the carving of the riverbed. I felt ready for heaven. Yet, I hadn't wanted to feel this ready this *soon*.

To live is Christ, to die is gain.

But to long is pain.

You Can't Stay

I felt the seizure building in my head—the pain, the fogginess, the tingling needles under my skin. My eyes faded and blurred, and I rose out of my body, my mind hovering over itself in a dark, elusive, prickling shadow. Darkness swelled in and out, breathing around my head. I couldn't move, the pain screamed, but no one could tell because I just lay there, motionless. The fear and panic built inside until the whirl of quiet sounds around me—the air conditioner humming, the fridge turning on, the touch of blankets, the plastic blinds on the window rustling as Colton climbed into bed next to me—drowned me, smothered me. I groped for air. The buzzing swallowed me. I still heard the sounds—loud, confusing, crashing like the swell of a nightmare. Colton sat next to me, but he felt far away, unreachable. I tried to move, to cry out—nothing. Then, suddenly, no air.

I felt Colton grab my arm, but I couldn't wake up, couldn't respond to him. His voice came from far away, "Sydney? Sydney?" He thrust a finger under my nose, then felt for my pulse.

"Nope. No." His voice grew rigid with panic. "You're not doing this. We're not doing this." He pulled my body to a sitting position in the bed. My mind blurred and panicked into silence. I tried to inhale, willing my lungs to pull the air down and expand, but my throat clenched. A choking inside stifled me, closing my airway.

"Sydney!" Colton shouted. He pulled my shirt down low on my neck and raked his knuckles across my sternum. Pain shot through me, and my lungs inhaled. I gasped as if I had been pulled out of water.

"Wake up. Wake up, Sydney." I could hear him fumbling with the blankets, the creak of the bed frame, and his frantic stumbling out of the room into the bathroom. The faucet ran. My eyes stayed shut. I inhaled—a raspy, shallow wheeze—barely. I felt cold water being splashed across my face, up my nose, down my throat. I gasped again, and my eyes opened. Colton stared at me.

"You stopped breathing," he said. "You stopped breathing." I sank forward into his chest and he held me, stroking my hair.

"You stopped breathing, Sydney."

I couldn't speak. I sagged into him, feeling the breath go in and out of my lungs, remembering when it stopped.

"Listen. I'm going to tell you something, and you're not going to argue with me about it." He pulled back and made me look at him, holding my shoulders in both his hands. "You can't get the care you need here. It's taking too long to get you on my military insurance, and we can't get you a specialist soon enough. We've been to the ER three times. You can't stay here."

I nodded. This was serious, but at the time, it didn't seem real. It all felt distant, dreamlike, heavy; the world was falling asleep around me, and I was sinking in the middle of it.

"I can't get leave soon enough to make this happen, but you still have your old medical coverage in Washington. You need to fly back without me. For however long it takes. We're getting this figured out."

My dad flew from my hometown in Poulsbo, Washington, all the way to Fort Riley, Kansas, just to fly right back with me. The wheelchair jolted over the jet bridge threshold as the airline assistant pushed me toward the plane, my dad walking next to us, carefully supervising.

"So . . . what's wrong with you?" the assistant asked bluntly. She probably wasn't used to pushing people my age.

"Jury's still out," I said.

My hands trembled in my lap, curled and cold. My husband was back there in Junction City, Kansas, and I was flying away from him. I hadn't realized the dependence these last few weeks had created in me. He felt like my only safe place. I was leaving my strong arms behind.

The flight attendants greeted me with plastic smiles, eyeing my young, apparently healthy body up and down. I could not reply. My voice had gone. I was the wordless woman in seat 14A, clutching a bottle of water I couldn't open, with legs that couldn't move, and a body that didn't always know how to breathe on its own. I was being sent away—not because I wasn't loved but because I was. There is a certain helplessness in the face of that kind of love. You can't argue against love like you can hatred. You can only surrender.

I spent the flight leaning against the window, confused thoughts rising to the surface of my mind. *We are not moving, but the ground is moving. The ground is shaking. The road is running away.* I remained coherent enough to vaguely know not to say these things out loud, but not coherent enough to silence the jumbled voice in my mind. A ground assistant waved to me through the window before we took off. *He doesn't know I'm dying or that I need a cane and wheelchair,* I thought. *It's nice when people don't know.*

There was no surge of courage, no sudden sense of peace. Just survival. Strong arms behind me. But God's stronger arms beneath me. Actual upholding arms, actual keeping arms, with actual breath-entering-lungs mercy. God pursues us even when we feel we are being carried away. He sometimes pursues us loudly—but most times, His pursuit is quiet. The quiet faithfulness of a God who does not lose track of His children, even when they are limp and voiceless and scattered in body and soul. He doesn't wait for us to rally, doesn't demand we steady our voices or our limbs or our thoughts or even our spiritual states before He draws near to us. Even to airport wheelchairs, and to grimy tiled floors. Even to seat 14A.

The walls breathed, and I lay between them. Hallucinating waves—the walls and floor swelling with air and deflating again. Colton stayed on the phone as I went in and out of seizures. Before I went under again, I said, "Please, *please*, can you come? Something is so wrong." I felt worse, weaker—more confused—every day.

I barely remember the MRI. I remember not feeling all the way there. I remember being so sick the receptionist's voice filled with audible relief when she found a space for me. I remember the walls and thinly carpeted floor of the waiting room, swelling and deflating like the walls of my bedroom. The lab tech watched as staff lifted me from the hospital wheelchair to the MRI cot. He put a hand on my shoulder.

"It's gonna be okay," he said. Weakness drained me of an answer. I could hear in his tone that he saw the severity of my symptoms. Relief settled over me at being taken seriously without needing to fight for it. My eyes stared, seeing without seeing. I counted the seconds between the beeps in the MRI machine to determine what had passed. The machine clacked and racketed around me—why did I think an MRI was quiet? The clatter crashed into my head, my body screamed, blind, convulsing.

"Lie still, ma'am. Please try to lie still." The voice came through the speaker, overlaying the Brad Paisley country station they had playing. I tried to turn my attention from the machine's angry rattle to the music. I tried to focus my eyes on the ceiling of the tube: *Just look at that screw. Look at that screw.* But now I saw two screws, side by side, shifting, floating apart and snapping together, like magnets fighting poles. The screws wavered and blurred, crashing into one again as my eyes rolled back and I convulsed. I could feel more than see the plastic cage around my head. Apparently, brain disorders and claustrophobia don't mix. The words of Christ echoed in my mind: "When you were younger, you girded yourself and walked where you wished; but when you are old, you will stretch out your hands, and another will gird you and carry you where you do not wish" (John 21:18).

Jesus spoke those words to Peter—words of sorrow, of prophecy, of love. He was speaking of the way Peter would die—on a cross, upside down, because Peter would think it too great an honor to die in the same manner as his Savior. *You will stretch out your hands, and another will carry you where you do not wish.*

I didn't want to be here. I didn't want my body to break, my mind to fracture, my world to blur into seizures and silence and sterile rooms. I didn't want this MRI tube, these panicked prayers, this helpless floating through pain and unpredictable suffocation.

But I was not alone—no matter how much I felt it. And neither are you.

You are not alone in the MRI tube, in the hospital room, in the quiet house where your body is falling apart. You're not alone sitting before the phone that never rings, the bank account verging on empty, the car forever in the shop. You are not alone though your spouse left you, though your children forsook you, though the church that was supposed to lead you closer to Christ tore you apart. You are not alone in the places where fear replaces breath, or when you cannot cry for help because your voice won't come.

Sometimes—in fact, more often than not—the greatest act of faith is not marching triumphantly forward, but rather lying still in the tunnel, staring at screws that blur and split, and whispering through cracked lips, "Still, I trust You. *Even here.*"

"I know this is hard—unimaginably hard," my dad had said on the way to the hospital. "But you need to trust Jesus with this too. You can still have hope, and joy, in this suffering."

"I do!" I said. "I am so ready for whatever comes." I believed it. But I really meant I was ready to die, ready for this to be over. I couldn't bear the thought of living.

Strength for Today

I sagged over the desk in my old bedroom, staring into the mosaic mirror I'd crafted as an eight-year-old. A gaunt, hollow-eyed reflection stared back at me. My hair lay in black, frizzy tangles around my pale, thin cheeks. Acne and blemishes blotted my skin—always one of my first signs of restricted calories. But most different—my eyes. Dilated, dull, devouring themselves with exhausted desperation. Dark circles pooled beneath them, the only shading of my pallid skin. My eyes looked so far away, like my mind, my body, my life.

I opened my phone and scrolled through our wedding photos, taken just weeks before. I looked at the bright, sunshiny face in the pictures, the happy brown eyes that beamed up at her new husband. The photos were beautiful, capturing the sunlight streaming through my white tulle dress and veil, my skirts sweeping around me as I swished and twirled—reveling in the fulfillment of perhaps every little girl's dream of feeling like a princess.

I was in pain then too, I reminded myself. I swayed on my feet through the ceremony, trying to soak in my father's words as he married us, all the while praying I could stand until the end. Relief washed over me when I could pass my bouquet to my sister—the matron of honor—and turn to face the strong man beside me. Colton held my hands in his in traditional wedding fashion, and I clung to his support, hoping no one would notice how much I fought to stay upright. I thanked God for the first time that Washington's pandemic restrictions forced our gathering to be small. We were married in a church elder's living room with just our two immediate families and grandparents.

Colton and I walked down the living room aisle together, out the front door, and into the driveway stacked with family cars. We shared our first private kiss between the gray and red Chevys. I touched up my lipstick afterward in the garage.

My sister made a dark chocolate cake and adorned it with red roses. My younger sister twirled in her pink flower girl dress—delighting as a five-year-old in the same princess sensation I enjoyed in my wedding gown. We signed the marriage license on the kitchen counter across from the dishwasher. Then Colton carried me out of the room to the send-off of our parents, grandparents, and siblings. My grandma's Honda Civic idled in the driveway with white chalk hearts painted over the windows. I waved goodbye and blew a kiss to my family, who then went back inside to fold up the few chairs, load the wooden sign and faux flowers from Joann Fabrics, and unwrap the tulle from the living room stairwell.

Colton and I made it through our wedding pictures, and once again, relief flushed through me every time I could lean into Colton's strength, letting him hold me through the poses our photographer suggested. I feared this chronic pain, which had whittled my body down to skeletal thinness over the last several months, would one day tire Colton of being the support I clung to.

Turning from the wedding pictures on my phone to the smudged, six-inch mosaic mirror in my old bedroom, I wanted to laugh. That fear seemed petty and childish now in light of the wasted twenty-two-year-old who stared back at me. *Had he waited a few weeks, he could have escaped this mess,* I thought. *Now, either way, death or no death, sick for life or sick to dying, he will suffer. I hate that. I hate it as much as I hate my own pain. It is so unfair. But I need him. I need him so much. And that is unfair too.*

My parents often reminded me that God promises strength for tomorrow, but He only gives you strength for today. If you consider the years stretching ahead in your life, you may think: *How, Lord? How will I get through this?* You find the answer in looking to Him, not the length of your years. Take this next breath in faith. You cannot live through tomorrow's pain yet, nor has God given you the strength for it yet. But when tomorrow comes, His strength will be there, just as it held you today.

If only I could've felt it then. For a moment. If only I could've felt what I knew to be true.

Even in this darkness, separated from my husband, isolated from the world, my life, my own body, God sent glimmers of grace to strengthen me. Twice, this happened at my weakest: lying in bed, floating in and out of coherence, blind to everything beyond the violent convulsions of pain and the hallucinations that surrounded me whenever I dared to open my eyes.

My mom crept into the room, sat beside me on the bed, held my hand, and closed her eyes, praying, swaying, and rocking. Sometimes she whispered or murmured broken pleas on my behalf. Other times her voice trailed off into a yearning silence. I could barely see her as my body twisted itself around the throes of agony. Yet I knew she prayed for me, and I knew I had never seen anyone pray for me like that before, except my husband. She didn't try to speak to me, and I couldn't have spoken back or acknowledged her if she had. Then she pressed my hand and slipped out of the room again, as the walls and ceiling spun inward to fill her void.

The Lord gave me relief after that—a short, peaceful respite from the writhing and contortions. I even managed to limp out to the living room, giving a wan smile for the first time since I'd left Colton behind in Kansas. My mom's face shot up, lighting with surprise and joy at seeing me on my feet.

"Thank you for praying for me," I whispered. "I can't stay out here, but I wanted you to know that God answered it and has given me relief right now." I went back into the room and crawled into bed. Colton called a few minutes later and said he had gotten leave—he would be with me in three days.

The Bridegroom

A heartbeat of hope now pulsed beneath the agony: *Colton is coming. Colton is coming.*

No longer did the hours and days stretch forward into a horizonless realm of suffering. Somehow—though I understood Colton couldn't bring healing with him—I could tell myself: *I only need to hold on for three more days.* I would be with my husband again, and with his presence, I wouldn't feel alone in whatever happened next. He would advocate for the testing I needed and help me sort through the doctors' visits. He would be with me for whatever news arrived. He would hold me through my seizures and comfort me when I became frightened and confused.

Pain still ravaged me, fragility left me bedridden, and seizures and hallucinations still swelled the walls of the room; but knowing Colton was coming changed the way I endured each hour. It gave me a focus and a strength I hadn't been able to muster on my own. My bridegroom was returning to me, and with his coming came hope.

Colton's return was a promise, but it was just a shadow of the greater promise—the greater return of the Bridegroom yet to come. Colton's imminent arrival didn't remove my pain, but it changed it. His nearness didn't make me well, but it gave me a future point in time to hold on to. That future hope—magnified, concentrated, glorified—is what the coming of Christ promises to those who trust in Him. The future coming of Christ doesn't end your pain now, but its promise changes the way you suffer.

Some kinds of suffering make you scan the horizon. Your eyes search ahead, looking for a distant sail, a rescuer, off the island of your pain. Intense suffering can strip you of pretense, performance, distraction until all that is left is a whispered, "Come, Lord Jesus" (Revelation 22:20). I used to read that verse with excitement. Now I read it with an ache. Every Sunday in church, I lift the communion cup with the whispered word, "*Maranatha!* Come quickly, Lord Jesus! Lord Jesus, come!" I read Revelation 22:20 with my whole body now. It is the cry of the weary pilgrim, the riven soul, the trembling saint. It is the thought-prayer of the bedridden and the brokenhearted. *Come quickly, Lord Jesus. Lord Jesus, come!*

Amid all our deepest suffering on this earth, we await the Bridegroom. Titus 2:13 says that as we live in this present world, we are "looking for the blessed hope and glorious appearing of our great God and Savior Jesus Christ."

Five years ago, I was waiting for Colton's presence to share the burden of my suffering. But *every day* of my life on this earth now and yet to come, I wait for my Savior who will bear it all away. The Bridegroom who *does* bring healing with His arrival. The Bridegroom who rips apart the sky as a curtain, to step into sterile rooms and whispered prayers and seizures and silence. The Bridegroom who comes as a Lamb and a Lion, with love and triumph. The Bridegroom who will never grow weary of holding us up.

A few hours after my mom left my bedroom, pain once again racked my body and convulsions writhed me in spasms of agony. My dear friend Heidi walked into the room with a P. G. Wodehouse book tucked under her arm.

"You don't have to say anything," she said. "I'm just here to read to you and maybe provide a little distraction."

She sat down on the rolling desk chair and opened the book. Her voice filled the small room with the cheerful, homelike words of one of my favorite authors. Every few minutes my body would convulse, and my breathing would labor into a shallow wheeze. I would sometimes hear Heidi's voice catch a little when this happened and feel her eyes on me, watching the contortions of pain. Then she would pause as if to collect herself and start reading again, picking up from where she left off. I have no idea which stories she read or how long she sat there—perhaps hours. But I know she sat, that she spoke another voice into the room besides the screaming of my own mind. I don't even remember if I could thank her, but I cried thankfulness to God after she left.

The offerings of prayer and P. G. Wodehouse had strengthened my heart.

And my Bridegroom was coming.

FIVE

pain

I sat in the waiting room, clutching the new plastic fold-up cane my dad had picked up from Walmart, and watched the hallucinations. It was one day after my MRI appointment, and I was still staying at my parents' house, waiting for Colton to arrive from Kansas. But today, I had been able to get a last-minute appointment with a local neurologist, and I was pretty sure this would fix everything. Today, I would have a name for what was wrong with me. Today, I would know my pain.

The middle-aged neurologist gave me a quick visual once-over. His green eyes—set beneath brown-gray hair and a trimmed beard—never met mine. I sat next to my dad, anxious but hopeful, and told the neurologist about the progression of symptoms over the last few weeks. His calmness was reassuring, as if he already knew what was wrong with me. I clung to that.

"Walk down there for me," he said, gesturing outside the room. I looked down the long hallway, a distance that would have seemed impossible on most recent days. My legs could support me today;

they were not paralyzed, but they were ataxic. Each step demanded painful, exhausting, ludicrous effort. My torso would swing first, one arm holding the cane, the other jerking back and forth in the air at my side. Then one leg would lift—not from the knee, but from the hip, stiff and awkward, as the other shuddered and buckled beneath my weight. For a few seconds, I would stand there unbalanced, stiff, swaying, as my brain fought to lower my leg again. My lifted leg would swing and spasm out to the side, and then drop. Then my other knee would buckle. I would pause, catching my breath, and focus hard to bring my next leg up from the hip, while my torso started its precursory jerking. One step.

I made it down the whole hallway like that. I hoped each jolting stride was carrying me closer to answers, closer to never needing to walk like this again. Halfway through the way back, the neurologist turned and went into the room as if bored, as if he'd already seen enough. I had the queer feeling that a key witness had left the courtroom.

By the time I tottered back into the room, he had taken a seat, tablet in hand. "I know what you have," he said. "Functional neurological disorder. It's caused by buried trauma and anxiety. Very common in women who have suffered abuse in the past."

I stared at him, the words colliding in my brain. Trauma? Anxiety? What was he talking about?

"I haven't been abused," I whispered.

He leaned back in his chair. "Then it's probably from some other buried trauma. Like I said, very common in women."

Very common in women? This didn't feel like a diagnosis, but a categorical dismissal. I wanted to hit him.

Pain had been rotting my body, sharper and more relentless than anything I had ever imagined. My legs had refused to carry me. I had been collapsing into unconsciousness without warning, my breathing failing, and entire pieces of my body—speech, taste, movement—slipping out of my control in erratic and unpredictable episodes. Most days, I couldn't leave my bed, writhing in agony, my body a prisoner to its own chaos. My life had ground to a halt, every moment—every inhale and exhale—a thing to endure. And this was because I was female?

"Did you look at my brain scans?" I said, trying to keep my voice steady.

The neurologist looked annoyed. "Oh . . . no, I didn't."

"Can you look at them, please?"

"Sure." He opened the tablet on his lap and flicked through the pictures. "Nothing of concern," he said.

"My primary care doctor said my brain scans showed abnormal white matter."

"Well, yes, there is some of that," he admitted. "But nothing of concern. Spots like that can be normal."

I blinked, struggling to process. Abnormal was, definitionally, *not normal*. "But . . . I can't *walk*," I said.

"Now we know why." He snapped the tablet shut and looked at my dad, who was next to me, listening. "It looks like your primary care doctor here ordered further STAT scans of your spinal cord to check for MS. No longer necessary. I'm canceling those and writing you a referral to a psychologist."

I stared at him, too angry to speak. He glanced at me. "A lot of people are upset when I give them this diagnosis," he said, as if accepting this as a sad part of life. "The receptionist will give you a referral form for that psychologist in Bremerton."

I couldn't move. My dad murmured a thank-you for me as we left. I stayed quiet, fuming, on the drive home. When we got to the door, my mom let us in.

"So? What did he say?"

"He said I have anxiety," I snapped.

Her face fell. "What? But how could that be?"

"I don't know. He's a quack."

I stumbled to my bedroom, then collapsed into bed as tears erupted from me. I convulsed, the sobs merging with the spasms I couldn't control. Our horrors must be named, if only to make them something we can talk about—something we can hold in our hands, examine, grieve, suffer. Without a name, pain is a ghost. Untouchable. Unprovable. Easy for others to dismiss and for ourselves to question. We ache for language to make our pain real, to make it exist outside ourselves. If you've ever sat with your own ache, physical or emotional, and whispered, "What is happening to me?"—then you know this. I *needed* a diagnosis. And this couldn't be it.

The next few days were a constant battle of seizures and phone calls. I first tried to call the place where I had been scheduled for spinal cord scans: "I'm sorry, those have been canceled," the receptionist said. "You need to call your primary doctor who ordered them."

I called my primary doctor. She wouldn't speak to me, but her assistant explained: "The neurologist who diagnosed you said those were no longer necessary, so we've pulled those referrals. We do have a referral to a psychologist for you. You can call and schedule that, if you like."

I would not like. I called the neurologist's office. "I recently received a diagnosis there, but the neurologist canceled all my other scans," I said. "I am still experiencing a lot of symptoms, and I would like to reschedule those scans, please."

"I'm sorry, that's not possible," the receptionist said. "The neurologist said he wrote you a referral for treatment."

"Yes, to a psychologist," I vented. "But I can't *walk*."

After everything—after fighting for an appointment, after collapsing again and again without explanation, after finding just enough strength to believe that maybe, *finally*, we could find out what was wrong with me—the diagnosis was a door slammed in my face.

This kind of hurt can crawl, roach-like, into your sense of self.

This kind makes you question your sanity and strength in the same breath. It makes you wonder if *you* are the problem—if your pain isn't as real as someone else's since it doesn't scan well or show up on your blood test. Maybe you've sat in a paper gown under fluorescent lights, wondering if your body is lying to you, or if everyone else just refuses to listen. Maybe you've flicked open your patient portal to see your test results, only for your heart to sink at everything reading "within normal range." Not because you *want* to be sick—but because you *are* sick, and you need to know why. You need to name the horror. You need to pin the ghost.

My neurologist hadn't *seen* me. Not really. He hadn't seen the girl who used to run, who could barely even cross a room now. He hadn't seen the seizures that stole my speech, the nights I stopped breathing, the body that betrayed me daily. He saw a woman with a cane who seemed obviously troubled—and decided she was fragile, not sick. But I wasn't asking him to fix me. I was asking him to believe me.

We know a diagnosis is a name, but it's also permission. Permission to be taken seriously. Permission to seek help. Permission to stop blaming yourself. When you're sick and scared and unheard, that name becomes a lifeline. And I felt that doctor took that from me. I wanted the dignity of being believed.

Too many people I know have experienced this treatment in a doctor's office. Maybe you've sat on that sterile hospital cot, fighting back tears while a stranger handed you a flimsy answer and sent you home in pieces—told you your pain is in your head, or due to anxiety or stress, that your physical symptoms are caused by mental symptoms and therefore, somehow, not real. In the face of that, dismissal feels like more than a medical misunderstanding. It feels like the echo of every time you've ever told yourself to keep your suffering quiet, to push through, to somehow make it go away. How can you feel seen by God when the doctor right in front of you won't even meet your eye?

I didn't need someone to tell me I had anxiety; of course I did. My symptoms were pretty anxiety-inducing! I needed someone to validate that my pain was real. That it mattered.

An Embarrassing Need for Air

One week ago, the ER doctor in Junction City had told me this still-undiagnosed condition could kill me. My emergency-level symptoms had forced me away from my husband on an abrupt trip back to Washington. The receptionist at radiology had sighed with relief over the phone when she found a place for me. The MRI tech had squeezed my shoulder, concern etched on his face. The radiologist had spoken of abnormal white brain matter while I sat in a wheelchair, watching the floors and walls and ceiling swell and deflate around me. Every person had scrambled to help me, to match the seriousness of my symptoms with deliberate attention. Until, that is, a middle-aged neurologist with poor online ratings had diagnosed me with an apparently feminine condition: functional neurological disorder (FND).

I didn't feel like a person with a diagnosis. I felt like a problem no one wanted to solve. Once the neurologist labeled me as someone with FND, every medical support vanished. The doctors who had been racing to help me days before now remained aloof and disinterested. The urgency—the rushing to appointments, the worried expressions of specialists and technicians—had evaporated. A cold dismissal slid into their place, a sense that I had wasted their time.

Suffering is like being out of breath on a run. It happens to everyone, but no one talks about it. We want to pause when no one is looking, bend over double, heave, and wheeze alone. It is embarrassing to us—to need air. Let others see our steady pace, measured breathing, grim determination. Let them see our endurance. But let's *not* let them see our *need* to endure. That's the irony, isn't it? Our picture of endurance is anything but *real enduring.*

We think endurance means hard things don't touch you. That your child's diagnosis doesn't leave you clutching your ribs. Your spouse's affair doesn't knock the wind out of you. Your miscarriage doesn't slow your stride. Your symptom flare-up doesn't leave you drowning. We want to carry on as usual. When we are running out of air, we want to keep going as if we don't need it; weak people need oxygen, we think. Unfit people. Out-of-shape people. Real athletes *endure.* The needs of mere mortals don't touch them.

The problem is all of us are mere mortals. Even those you never see gasping for air have done so on occasion. When you find someone—a running partner, for instance—before whom you can gasp and wheeze like an old accordion staggering with a tune, you have found true gold. You can show your vulnerability, your humanness, your *unfitness.* You can show your need for air. And they show you theirs: "It's all right. I need it too. It's not embarrassing."

But there's always a risk. Sometimes you think you've found someone, and you take the plunge for the first time—you slow down, ludicrously out of breath, stripped of pretense. But what if they keep going without you? You look ahead and see the cloud of dust, and you are lost in the feeling of being left behind. The sting of abandonment, being left alone with your embarrassing vulnerability.

I replayed the neurologist's words over and over in my mind. Was I exaggerating? Was I making this all up? These doctors weren't just my running companions. They were my *coaches.* I shouted, desperate for them to hear me, to see me, to care enough to wait—but they didn't break stride. They didn't look behind them. "Deal with it," their fading backs seemed to say. "Push through by yourself, you damnable weakling."

Often, the ones you trust to support you most—a friend, a family member, a church leader, a doctor—become part of the most devastating losses. And yet. Even in that loneliness, there is hope. There is One who doesn't leave, who doesn't turn His back, who doesn't see you as unworthy. He doesn't tell you to figure it out alone. When you are gasping for air, beaten down by your suffering, it is tempting to conclude that God is angry with you or has abandoned you altogether. But what if your trials were intended to reveal something else? What if your need for air is not an accident but by design? What if, through your weakness, God is carving a void He wants to fill with Himself?

"It's okay. It isn't embarrassing. I AM the air."

Unseen

I lay on the bed in my grandparents' guest quarters and stared up at the ceiling. I could hear Colton next to me, tapping at the keys of the laptop. We had moved here after his arrival in Washington. Our reunion had been sweet and beautiful, but it hadn't brought the sudden change for the better I had dreamed of. I still drowned, still seethed, still felt strangely alone.

The familiar buzzing darkness began crowding in over my head. I slid into the seizure, my lids closed over my backward-rolling eyes, the usual outward spasms shuddering inside me. I couldn't move but could hear the laptop keys' continued tapping.

Usually Colton could see a seizure coming before I could. He always stopped what he was doing and held me, read Scripture to me, helped bring me back if the seizure took too long. This time, he didn't sense it. I lay right next to him, and he didn't know.

The minutes slid by, and I stayed under. I felt as if, underneath the dark paralysis, I awoke. My thinking became lucid again. I could hear Colton next to me, but I couldn't open my eyes, couldn't speak, couldn't move beyond a slight twitch in my forefinger. I used it to try to get his attention.

Tap-tap-tap. Tap. Tap. Tap. Tap-tap-tap.

God assures us that those who seek Him through faith and trust in His promises will never be deprived of what is truly good. Psalm 34:10 says, "The young lions suffer want and hunger; but those who seek the LORD lack no good thing" (ESV). I couldn't see it though. *Lord, what is this "good thing" You are giving me? I feel nothing good in my life. I see nothing good in my circumstances. Where is the fulfillment of Your promise?*

I continued tapping the SOS signal into the mattress, over and over. Colton noticed my finger twitching and grabbed my hand, squeezed it, and set it down again. Through all my jerks, twitches, and spasms, why would he assume this little finger was tapping for help? The computer keys continued.

What if the "good thing" God promises isn't a change in your circumstances but the gift of Himself? What if your hunger—for relief, for answers, for healing—isn't a robbery but a signpost, leading you toward the Bread of Life? What if the depth of your loss is not the end, but a painful, needful tug toward the place where God is offering you Himself?

"I say to the LORD, 'You are my Lord; I have no good apart from you'" (Psalm 16:2 ESV).

Tap-tap-tap.

"Whom have I in heaven but You? And there is none upon earth that I desire besides You" (Psalm 73:25).

Tap. Tap. Tap.

"Indeed, I count everything as loss because of the surpassing worth of knowing Christ Jesus my Lord" (Philippians 3:8 ESV).

Tap-tap-tap.

I wish I could say that amid that desolation, I remembered those truths. That those promises whispered comfort to me, that I clung to the good thing God promised. I wish I could say I thought of those verses or that I recognized, even in my despair, the love of a Savior who would never leave me.

But I didn't. I tapped and tapped my feeble plea. My desperate persistence felt more real than the presence of a persistent God.

The episode lasted three hours. The entire time, my ears were trained to the tapping of the computer keys, the slightest movement from Colton. I could feel him sometimes pausing and studying my face. I kept hoping he would see I wasn't asleep, that behind my closed eyelids and mouth I was panicked, trapped, and terrified. But how could he see? No other episode had presented in this way. As I lay suffocating and overwhelmed beneath the dark stillness of my body, I felt more and more alone. I became angrier, grew more fearful. *Surely, after this long, he must realize something is wrong.*

He had always recognized my symptoms before—even better than I had. He saw seizures in my eyes, could hear the catch in my voice before the convulsion happened. He checked my pulse and my breathing when I lay still for too long, worked movement back into my arms and legs, could see in my face when I needed him to carry me to a bed or couch to rest. But here I lay, trapped in one of my longest, most terrifying episodes yet, while he sat right next to me. And he didn't know.

If I could just blink. If I could open my eyes, I thought, straining my mind and focus to lift the clamped lids. For a long time, I struggled. Muscles I hadn't even known were there twitched above my eyelids. I tried to breathe. I thought: *Why is it so hard to blink and breathe at the same time?* One lid cracked, then closed again. The blurred slit of light that appeared for a moment drove me onward. I felt the weight of each minute as it passed by. Then my eyelids heaved up and open. Blurry colors shifted in and out of focus. I could see.

Colton only noticed something was wrong when he saw me glaring at him.

"Babe, are you okay?" He snapped the laptop shut.

About time, I thought.

"What is the matter? Why are you looking at me like that?"

I couldn't speak, but all my anger, terror, and frustration were in my eyes. Here, at last, I had one way to communicate, and all I wanted to communicate was rage.

"I thought you were sleeping long, but you were so tired," Colton said. "I didn't want to wake you."

I looked down at my finger—the only part of me, other than my eyes, that I could still move. I rapped it on the bed, then looked up at him again.

"Were you trying to talk to me?"

Glare.

"I thought you had another twitch like you get sometimes. Do you want me to help you move?"

Glare.

"That's a yes, I think." He chuckled, then moved the blankets off my legs. They were stiff, twisted, and ice-cold.

"Can you wiggle your toes for me?"

When I didn't answer, he crawled down to the end of the bed and wiggled my toes back and forth with his fingers. Then he lifted my feet and circled each ankle, working his way up my legs, trying to rub life back into my dead frame. Each time he moved a part of me, pain like electricity shot through my body and sent me into convulsions. It hurt so much to have my body *moved*. How would I ever move it on my own?

After another hour of this, after we had worked minimal movement back into my arms and legs, Colton pulled me to a sitting position, and I slumped against the pillows. The memory of those hours still terrified me.

I started crying. "When have I ever slept like that? When have I ever slept on my back, without moving, for hours? How did you not know something was wrong?"

"Babe, I'm sorry." Colton paused, searching my face. It seemed to dawn on him that bringing movement back into my limbs did *not* make everything right with the world. "This is new to me too. I'm figuring all this out for the first time like you are. You can't blame me for what no one could know."

I knew he was right. But my anger burned for hours—the anger that comes from fear. How terrifying it is to reach the place where the people closest to you can't rescue you—where no doctor, no test, no word can untangle the suffocating fear and loneliness. This episode felt like the last dead end. No rescue—no doctor, no brain scan, no diagnosis, no rescuer. No one on earth, not even my husband, could see, could feel, could know, could understand. Terror gripped me at the thought. And anger.

But the worst still threatened. The shadow of Colton's deployment loomed over everything: a day that marched closer with every throb of pain, every seizure, every episode, every halted breath. A countdown accompanied the convulsions, the paralysis, the fear. Every time my body failed, every time new or raging symptoms confused and terrified me, the relentless question whispered: *How am I going to do this alone?*

That night, I threw the bedcovers back and groped for my cane on the floor. "I'm hurting too much to sleep right now," I said. "I'm going to sit in the living room."

Colton stared at me. "Is that because you're still upset at me?"

"No." I couldn't look at him. Tension laced every cell of my body. My muscles were spastic, curled inward. I couldn't straighten. I hobbled toward the door, the drama of my gait mocking my self-entitled gravitas. *This isolation, this fear, is a taste.* It only preceded the inevitability of further isolation and terror.

Colton folded his arms. "What if you have another episode? I won't know."

"It wouldn't be the first time," I snapped. The words were cruel. I looked at him helplessly.

I know. I know you can't know. I know you couldn't know today.

But how will you know when you're gone? How will you know when five thousand miles separate us instead of the hallway and a door? What will happen if I'm alone and this happens again? Will I stop breathing one day and never restart? Will I lie paralyzed with no one to see or help me? How can I be this debilitated, this broken, this helpless and scared, while facing nine months of isolation as if nothing is wrong?

I didn't want to be alone. But solitude shadowed me. It's human nature, I suppose, to pull back when you're hurting, to shield yourself from the sting of disappointment. You withdraw from people you love because it feels safer than being let down. You build walls because the fear of being unseen—or worse, brushed aside—pierces your courage.

As a small child, I found comfort in knowing that God sees everything. He saw when I hid under my blankets from the shadows cast by the clothes hanging over the chair in my bedroom, and when those boys teased me for riding my bicycle with my new pink helmet and elbow guards. I pictured Him smiling when I poured Frosted Flakes into a plastic bowl for my little sister, or when I ran outside on a Thanksgiving night with my entire extended family, my Hawaiian *pareo* wrapped around my shoulders to see our first mainland snow. Kid stuff. God was there. God saw. I imagined Him like a benevolent grandfather in the sky, looking down with a smile and a host of angels, holding my hand through the unknown-to-me paths of the day.

As a kid, I had a recurring dream every Halloween. I was playing on a swing set (my favorite part of every playground), and my parents were sitting side by side on a park bench, watching me. They looked so happy, so proud. But when the swing took me high and I could see behind them, I saw a giant ice monster stomping toward the park.

I tried to stop the swing, but it kept moving—back and forth, up and down. Each time it rose, I could see the monster drawing closer, while my parents' smiling faces remained unaware of the danger behind them. Right as my shoe got a sliding, desperate hold on the turf below me and stopped the swing, my warning scream would catch in my throat. The ice monster would stomp down on my parents, leaving them frozen on the bench, still smiling. Then I would wake up.

I dreaded Halloween for years, afraid of that ice monster and also afraid to tell anyone about my dream because I was embarrassed. As a big girl I knew, of course, that "monsters aren't real." But as I got older and my knowledge of my own brokenness increased, I stopped fearing the costumes of trick-or-treaters outside my window. The God who saw all things felt far more fearsome. There were corners of myself I wanted to hide. Monsters *were* real, after all. And they weren't outside at the park or lurking in my bedroom; they were inside me. I was the one who hurt people I loved. I couldn't stop bad things from happening. What if I wasn't the scared child on the swing set but the monster that ruined everything in its path?

The taunts I faced weren't from bullies but from the whispers inside my own mind. Anger, impatience, bitterness, depression, fear, and doubt kept my conscience in constant turmoil—a heartache of conviction without assurance.

I limped out to the living room, sat down on the palm-green sofa, and tried to calm the convulsions the effort caused. Isolation promises safety but delivers despair. Pulling away feels like control, but it is a false sense of security. Fear tells us we're better off alone, but the truth is we were never meant to be alone—even in Eden. Like Jonah fleeing from the path God set before him, we run. And God pursues. We are swallowed up by waves and monsters, and God pursues. We curse and grope at the loss of small things dear to us—and still, God pursues.

I heard rustling in the bedroom. The door snapped open.

"If you're sleeping out here, then I need to," Colton said.

"Don't bother."

"Then come to bed."

I faltered. "I can't."

"Fine. But this is ridiculous." He dragged the blanket up the stairs to the pullout couch. He sat down, the thin springs creaking in protest. "I can see you from here, so this is the best I can do."

"You don't have to sleep there!" I called after him, annoyed.

He didn't answer but pulled the blanket up and rolled over, facing the wall.

What is wrong with me? Why am I building a wall when I know Colton loves and cares for me? Is it all a game? A farce we play together? These symptoms are serious, and I need his help—so I'll pretend his deployment isn't coming? Pretend this will all end in a few months when Colton leaves? Pretend I'll suddenly be able to care for myself then? Pretend the inevitable isn't crawling closer with every pain-filled night like this one? Pretend today is the isolated event, not the precursor? Pretend today isn't the foretaste of what the future will be?

God, in His omniscience and His sovereignty, pierces the mask you hide behind. And still—*still*—this God who sees all things, in His omnipotent love and grace, sent His beloved Son to take on your flesh. To feel as you feel, suffer as you suffer, see as you see—yet without the blindness of sin. God looked upon His beloved Son, who upheld the whole law, and said: "This is My beloved Son, in whom [and in whom alone] I am well pleased" (Matthew 3:17).

And then, when Christ suffered the most pain, the most torment, the most anguish of any being in history before or since, the God who sees all things closed His eyes and turned away. When His perfect Son dangled on the cross for the sin God had abhorred for eternity, Christ screamed in agony: "My God, My God, why have You forsaken Me?" (Matthew 27:46).

God closed His eyes to His Son so He might never close His eyes to you. So that you will never be unseen. So that when He turns His gaze upon you, He sees His Son's own perfection, covering you like white robes.

That is the gospel.

Later that night, when some of the pain had subsided, I crawled up the stairs on my hands and knees and onto the pullout bed next to Colton. The bed seemed to retreat into the corner, and Colton slept smack in the center of the mattress, the only blanket twisted around his body. He assumed I would sleep downstairs in the big bed like a sane person. Or an angry wife. One or the other.

Ridiculous is right, I thought as the slant of the mattress rolled my body up against his. *How did we both end up crammed in here when there was a perfectly good and comfortable bed downstairs in the bedroom?*

The pain settled heavy upon me again. I stared at the ceiling, listening to Colton's breathing next to me. I tried to imagine silence. No breathing. Alone with my pain. Alone with the frozen statue of what I loved—and the monster.

On the nights you don't feel comforted, don't feel strong, and don't feel held, but instead feel yourself unraveling in the dark, know this: One day, this barren wilderness will erupt and bring forth the Water of Life. This foreign land will give way to your true home. One day, everything you want, you will have. You will see with your own eyes the God who sees. In the dark stillness no one else understands, He is there. And even when it doesn't feel like enough, He is still enough.

I wish I could go back and say that to myself then. Instead, my tears slipped onto the mattress, soaking into the narrow space between us.

SIX

disabled

I sat at my laptop at three in the afternoon in our Grandview Plaza apartment, staring at the black and red YouTube page on my screen. The video I had opened showed someone walking. Someone with functional neurological disorder. They were walking like me. Hip up, leg stiff and lifted, torso jerking, leg spasming to the side, then down again, buckling, one step, starting over. It was me. Just. Like. Me.

We were back in Kansas, ten weeks before Colton's deployment, and I had spent the last few days researching different types of gait ataxia—those caused by multiple sclerosis, Lou Gehrig's disease, cerebral palsy, brain damage, tumors, Parkinson's. Each disease presented gait ataxia in a different way. I didn't know there were so many ways to *not* be able to walk. Apparently I couldn't walk like someone with FND.

I snapped the computer shut and gazed at the bare apartment walls, then out the sliding glass door. The only window in our living room gaped, bare and curtainless. It looked out over a concrete slab and a narrow strip of dead grass, and straight into the gray walls of the apartment complex's storage units about six feet away. A thin line of blue sky stretched above the storage unit roof, about a foot long and six feet wide, blocked otherwise by the tin roof and the white frame of the sliding glass door.

When we got back from our honeymoon a month before, we found everything we had to start our new home—everything from the wedding registry gifts and my personal items I had sent ahead—had been stolen. The first night, in lieu of our now-stolen mattress, I stuffed the clothes we had packed for our honeymoon into empty pillowcases so we could sleep on the floor in Colton's Army sleeping bag. I grieved most, however, for my books. My Bible, my sketchbook and journal, all the classics I had gathered and curated over the years, read over and over, all the books most dear and important to me, were gone. They had no value except to me, so we spent weeks searching dumpsters in the surrounding neighborhoods, hoping the thief had simply thrown them away. We filed a police report, but nothing came of it.

We were scraping by, so we only bought the essentials—a small air mattress, a few pots and pans, and some eating utensils. We had no decorations, no furniture, no pictures, and one car. So I spent hours sitting on the floor by that sliding glass door, staring out the window at the strip of blue sky and wishing I could walk again to meet it. I remember searching online: "Is it possible to get depression from lack of colors?" I couldn't find a definitive answer, and the gray, bare emptiness around me took on the same vague gloom of every other unanswered question in my life. I stared out the window now, replaying in my head how that person in the video had walked. Did I . . . *Did* I have FND?

We never were able to reclaim those follow-up appointments in Washington. Every call was a dead end, so we headed back to Kansas, hoping to finish the process of transferring me to Army insurance and finding a specialist there. My hope and prayer was that I would be able to find a better doctor and get a "real diagnosis" before Colton left for his deployment and I returned to Idaho for my sophomore year of college. Thanks to my naive understanding of the medical industry, I was certain that a new place with new care would provide a fresh start—but the diagnosis followed me. The day before, I had received a call from the nearest neurological center in Kansas City, saying they would not take anyone with functional neurological disorder—not even for further testing.

I didn't want to have FND. I remembered the way the neurologist had explained it in Washington—a psychological illness distinctive to females, the result of trauma and anxiety, a physical stress response to emotional suffering. I *hated* that. I hated it with every fiber of my being. This was *not* stress. This was *real*. Something far outside my control. Not a mental problem but a brain problem. *Not my fault.*

How had I just woken up one morning and not been able to walk? Why could I speak sometimes and other times have to relearn speech like a small child? Why did pain creep through every part of my body? Why did I go unconscious with these stupid seizures?

I don't understand. I don't understand. I don't understand.

Everyone deals with stress and trauma. So why did mine manifest in this way, and other people's didn't? Why did it feel as though this wasn't an illness but a weakness—something too fragile, too delicate, too broken deep inside me? I didn't want to have some awful, degenerating illness. But I did want a real good reason for why I felt this way. But there I was: stressed, apparently. From something big, horrible, and worse than anyone else had ever experienced?

No. Just from my little life.

The symptoms lingered, and I hated that the more I researched, the more I became convinced that the dismissive neurologist was right: I had FND. All the symptoms fit—the ataxia, the seizure episodes, the neurological symptoms that overlapped so many other disorders, the drastic fluctuation of symptoms from day to day, the erratic and unpredictable episodes of paralysis, the incoherence.

I thought accepting a diagnosis would be comforting, but instead, it made me angrier with myself. And in a way, it made me more hopeless. *This* was how my body reacted to stress? Everyday stress? I knew the triggers, the flare-ups, and yet—I had to get through the day. I had to do normal people things. I had to cook, and clean, and study, and work, and make dinner, and do laundry, and go on trips, and see other people, and get into arguments, and make up afterward, and hear loud noises, and see bright lights. I had to. This was the cost of living. Not a high cost. Most people don't think twice about it. But it seemed that for me, living sucked all the life out of me. Even on good days I struggled, feeling as if I was tottering on the brink, wondering if how I felt was normal, or if I had just gotten used to living in pain.

Spitting on Love

"I don't want my life to be this way!" I sat on the kitchen counter in our small apartment, holding on to Colton, who stood in front of me. He had hoisted me onto the counter when my legs buckled next to the fridge, then guided my hands onto his shoulders for support so I could recover.

"The fact that I'm not dying makes this harder." My body started convulsing again, and I doubled over against Colton's chest. I drew in my breath in jerks, trying to regain mastery over the spasms across my core so I could speak.

"I still feel like I'm dying," I said, my voice breaking. "I still feel like I'm dying, but I'm not. And now I'm going to have to feel like I'm dying for the rest of my life." I looked at Colton's face, then down at the floor. The narrow, five-foot strip of yellow vinyl needed to be mopped. I hadn't been well enough to mop it. "It's too long," I said at last, dead, wooden. "A lifetime is too long to feel this way."

Colton looked at me. He knew how much I struggled. For the last few weeks I had limped around in a blur, moving my pain-filled limbs through a slow fog of compromised existence. I barely spoke. I couldn't remember the last time I'd smiled. I hated to think that maybe *this* was the best I might ever feel again.

Colton took my hand. "I know it's hard," he said, his eyes expressing hurt for me, his voice careful, tender, as he picked his way forward. "But . . . I don't understand. When we thought you were dying, you were so strong . . . even cheerful. You made jokes. You laughed with me. You prayed. You fought so hard. And now we know that you're *not* dying. That's *good* news. But it's like you've stopped fighting. Why?"

I stared at the edge of our kitchen floor, where the white baseboard met the dirty vinyl. The fridge hummed. I met Colton's gaze.

"It's so easy to be happy when you think you're close to heaven," I whispered. "It's so much harder now. Nothing has changed in how bad I feel, but now I know it won't end any sooner. This pain will be in me as long as I am alive." My voice faltered as grief squeezed my stomach. "And I might be alive for a long, long time."

Colton hugged me. "I'm thankful you will be here for a long time. Maybe it's selfish," he rushed on, "but I don't think it is. It's what God chose for you, not me." Then he paused, grabbing my arms and holding me back to look at me.

"Sydney. A few weeks ago, you were on my team. You were fighting right alongside me. But now I feel like I'm fighting for us alone. I'm fighting all my battles as your husband to help you, care for you, support you. Now I'm fighting your battles too." He leaned his elbows on the counter beside me and lowered his head. "I can't keep fighting for both of us," he said, in a tone more tired and helpless than I'd ever heard him use before. "*I can't.* It doesn't work that way."

My body began convulsing again, and Colton rose, lifting me up off the counter. He cradled me and carried me over to the living room. We lay down on the carpeted floor, lying on our backs, and I stared at the swelling of the ceiling, as familiar to me now as the drywall itself. My hands trembled, my core spasmed, my eyes blurred in and out of focus, but Colton breathed steady, anchoring me. His words lingered in my mind. I thought of the way he had leaned over the counter. He hadn't shown his exhaustion to me before. A rush of shame filled me.

The last few weeks, I had been wrapped up in my own pain, bent around myself, fixated on the agony of feeling like a dying person who wasn't dying. I wanted others—Colton—to know I still struggled, that my suffering was as immense and valid as it was before my diagnosis. I needed him to see this wasn't a happy ending. Living felt excruciating. I wanted that fact to be validated, to be wrapped tightly around my heart, to be wrapped tightly around his. Suffering yearns for a witness. We ache to be seen in our pain—not pitied or fixed, but *known*. To have someone sit beside the jagged edges of our existence and say, "I believe you. This is real. It sucks." Sometimes all we want is for people to acknowledge that what we're carrying is heavy. That it matters.

I clung to Colton as the only witness I trusted with my pain—all of it: the incoherent episodes, the sleepless nights, the bad dreams, the hallucinations, the seizures, the stumbling, the staggering gait, the weariness of life. With my fear, my pain, my grief, my depression, I begged for his witness. But in doing that—curling around my pain, refusing happiness, refusing gratitude—I hadn't realized what I was communicating to Colton. I thought I only revealed myself, my story, my struggle, my own tiny, hardened gloom. But I wasn't just talking about me.

Every time I chose to cling to bitterness and despair, I said something *about Colton*. With every self-centered, resentful action, I said, "What you're doing for me isn't enough. Not enough to make me happy. Not enough for me to be grateful. Not enough for me to feel well-loved. Not enough to fight. Not enough to want to stay." I wanted Colton to know how much I struggled. How hard I fought to live a life I didn't want. And while I thought I could carry on in my silent protest, my lack of fighting actually fought *against him*. My despair didn't sit idly by. It became an enemy.

Your grief, exhaustion, or quiet bitterness might feel passive at first—like something happening to you. But over time, it starts to shift. It begins to speak on your behalf. It shapes how you respond, how you withdraw, how you protect yourself. Despair wounds the sufferer, but it also frays the bonds that keep us tethered to one another. Sometimes, without realizing it, we let it desert our will, betray our own side, and become the enemy. Suddenly you're not facing your pain across the battlefield. You are being ripped open by your own bullets, holding the muzzle pointing into your chest.

The room remained quiet except for the sound of Colton's steady breathing. My tremors tightened into a low, rigid spasticity. I turned my head to look at him. His eyes were fixed on the ceiling. He didn't speak, but his presence assured me: quiet, steady, loving. What I wish I knew then, but hadn't realized yet, is that though my actions *were* saying something about Colton, on a far bigger, deeper level, they said the same things about God: "You are not enough. Not enough to make me happy. Not enough for me to be grateful. Not enough for me to feel well-loved. Not enough to fight for this life You have given me. Not enough to want to stay."

The truth is, suffering doesn't just belong to you. It spills onto the people around you, shaping their lives in ways you didn't choose and can't control. The way you handle suffering says something about them. And it says something about God. This can be hard to realize, frustrating even. You're probably thinking: *I didn't choose this!* But you didn't have to. It's part of the design. It is far, *far* bigger than you.

Your existence *testifies*. You are a witness to your neighbor of God's goodness, His sufficiency, His character. We say to God, "Of course, You're enough," while our lives—like a slap in the face of the husband who loves us—say, "I hate this." Our sin proclaims to God and to our neighbor that God is not enough to make us happy. That

God's promises are not enough for us to fight, to hope, to laugh, to pray, to eat dinner, to cry, to sing, to clean our house, to do laundry, to drive, to go to church, to keep getting out of bed every morning.

Alan Noble shares in his book *On Getting Out of Bed: The Burden and Gift of Living*: "The uncomfortable truth is that suicide becomes a slightly more viable option for people when someone they respect succumbs to it . . . You have the solemn responsibility and privilege to bear witness to the goodness of life by living despite suffering . . . You are not your own, and neither is your suffering . . . the greatest gifts are always also burdens."[1]

For weeks I had been consumed by my own despair, the gnawing fear that my life would always look this way. But lying on that carpeted floor in our bare-walled apartment, I decided to fight, if only not to spit on Colton's love for me. His love deserved a response, even if I could only manage the resolve to keep breathing.

In a far bigger way, though I did not know it then, I had to learn not to spit on God. I thought I was walking to *my* crucifixion. But I wasn't. Like He did for every broken Christian in the world and throughout history, He took up the cross *for* me. Every ache, every weight, every wound I felt—it all only trickled down from what He bore for me and let break Him. I did not die on the cross. I lay in the shadow of the cross. The cross's shadow stretched into my suffering to put an end to it forever—even if to my feeble frame bound in time, forever didn't feel soon enough. His death, His life, His resurrection, His promises. They were enough. They had always been enough.

Winston Churchill on eBay

Deployment loomed. Two months away. Then one month. I tried not to think about it, but its sickening terror kept me on the edge of anxiety. *This isn't getting any easier. How am I going to do this alone?*

I had figured out how to work around some of the physical symptoms. I walked when my pain and paralysis allowed, clinging to a green plastic broomstick with both hands. I would plant it a few feet ahead of me and then swing my legs in their stiff, roundabout way to catch up.

"This is my gondola!" I said as I swayed across the floor in the unique grab-and-pull fashion. Colton laughed.

"It's good to see you making jokes again." He grinned at me, happy, thankful.

Most of the time, my jokes felt fake. But they were a way to keep fighting, even when I struggled to laugh inside.

I moved our pots and pans to the kitchen floor and began prepping our food there, sitting cross-legged, peeling potatoes into the small plastic trash can under the counter. My method wouldn't have met food-safety code, but I found it necessary, and I never let any food or utensils touch the floor.

Once, my brain shut off my sense of taste without me realizing it. I added loads of salt to a ground turkey dish, wondering why the salt *wasn't salting.*

When I found out later what happened and told Colton, he said, "Thank *God.*"

I hadn't expected that. He started laughing with relief, looking at me apologetically.

"The food tasted so bad, Sydney. We've only been married a few weeks, and I couldn't help thinking: *What did I get myself into?*"

I laughed too. I couldn't help it. All this time, I had been worried Colton would have those very same doubts because I'd fallen sick, couldn't walk, was having seizures, and needed him so much. But the first and only time he'd entertained that thought had been because I'd oversalted ground turkey. *Lord,* I thought, *I have a good man.*

Another couple at Fort Riley was being stationed at a different fort in Missouri. They generously offered us the furniture they wouldn't be taking with them, and in one day we acquired our small, faux-leather, blue-green love seat, a queen-size mattress and black metal bed frame, and a wobbly four-person dining room table with a hinged leaf on the side and four wooden chairs. The addition of furniture to our apartment worked wonders. Even those small bits of vinyl, metal, and particle board were welcome relief after the bare and colorless rooms I had been trapped in for so long. I could sit on the couch now to stare out at my friendly strip of blue sky, sip tea in our new glass mugs, and think myself rich indeed—in everything but physical health.

Colton sat down on the couch one day and gestured to the spot next to him. I gondola-ed my way across the floor, and we grinned at the awkwardness of the silent wait before I reached him.

"What's up?" I said, placing my trusty broomstick on the carpet at my side.

Colton let out his breath and looked at me. "You know I'm going to be deployed soon."

My heart sank. I didn't want to talk about this. I didn't want to think about this. I nodded and looked away.

I hadn't ever taken my broomstick outside with me, for obvious reasons. When we went out together, I would cling to Colton's arm for support. The longer we were out, the more my gait would deteriorate. I would begin our outings looking like an affectionate, though perhaps overly clingy new wife who didn't want to let go of her husband's arm. After a while, I started to look more like an intoxicated wife being helped along the sidewalk by her husband.

"Darling, you need to curb this drinking problem," Colton said once as we shuffled past someone in our apartment hallway. I grinned in embarrassment, and my face turned red.

Colton laughed. "Sorry, couldn't help it," he whispered. "We gotta have fun with this *sometimes*."

Often, my legs would give out before we even made it across the parking lot or down the hallway to our apartment again. When this happened, Colton would have to lift me up, carry me inside, and lay me on the bed, where I could spend the rest of the day recovering.

"I'm leaving in a few weeks," Colton began again, squeezing my hand so I would look at him. He paused. "And I'm taking my arms with me."

I smiled despite myself. "How dare you?" I sighed, glancing up teasingly into his face.

Colton laughed, then paused again, letting out his breath. "I think we need to consider getting you a cane."

He could see it in my face: I hated this idea.

"I don't want a cane," I protested. "I will feel like . . . like *that's it.* Like I'm always going to be this way. I'll feel like . . . like an old person!"

Colton didn't laugh. He sat quietly, letting me finish.

"I looked up the definition of *disability* the other day," I said after a moment, not able to meet his gaze. "It's defined as 'any physical or mental condition that limits a person's movements, senses, or activities.'"[2] I paused and peeked at Colton's face. "Am I . . . *disabled*?"

Colton looked surprised for a moment, then recovered himself. "You have a physical condition that limits your movements, senses, and activities *every day*," he said carefully. He paused and squeezed my hand. "Yes, baby," he continued. "As long as your body is like this, you are disabled."

The word hung in the air. I had never let myself say it out loud before. *Disabled?* I was disabled. It seemed so final, so labeling. I had admitted I was sick. Even chronically ill. Chronically in pain. But disabled? I had not admitted that yet, even after my diagnosis, even as the debilitating symptoms had lingered for weeks and months. It astounded me even more that Colton seemed to have known this weeks ago. It seemed to bewilder him that I had only realized just then.

Disabled. I rolled the word over in my mind. Disabled like other people are disabled. Disabled like wheelchair users, and old people, and the injured, and the neurologically broken. The sort of people who hobbled along with a cane. My mind lingered over the gap, over the strange *otherness* that had always stood between me and those who were physically different. They *weren't* different. They were like me. They *were* me.

"I know you don't like the idea of getting a cane," Colton said, drawing my mind back to the conversation at hand. "But, babe, there are some cool canes out there! We can get you a really classic one—stylish even! A cane that would make Winston Churchill jealous." He paused, leaned over, and grabbed the laptop on the couch next to me.

"Look, look!" he exclaimed, typing "eBay" into the search engine. "Classic-style cane," he muttered as his fingers tapped the keys. "Look at all these!" He scrolled down the page, full of black wood and bronze, silver and gold handles. "Look at this one!" He clicked on one listing and opened the pictures, magnifying the image to show me the engravings on the handle, the designs etched into the wood. "These are cool! You won't look like you're old, or sick, or boring. You will look . . . *cool*."

I smiled, despite myself. I saw kindness in his excitement for me, in his efforts to make me excited, when he probably felt the difficulty of this step almost as much I did. He grinned and handed me the laptop.

"I want you to find one you *really* like," he said. "Price doesn't matter!" We looked at each other and laughed. Price definitely *did* matter.

"I'm serious, babe," he said more gently. "I want you to have a cane you really like, something you feel confident using. And I . . ." He squeezed my hand again. "I will feel so much better knowing you have one while I'm gone."

"Okay," I said, smiling back at him. I knew he was right. I *would* need a cane, and I might as well make the best of it.

I opened the web page again. "Winston Churchill canes," I typed into eBay.

Jeeves

Black and gold leaves encircled the staff of my new cane, all beneath a silver-engraved handle. "Help me name it!" I messaged my dear friend Heidi. "Naming it will make it feel better to use." The next day, she sent me a picture of an elaborate map of Post-it notes on her wall, full of dozens of brainstormed names, definitions, origins, and meanings. My heart warmed. She sent so much love in those colorful Post-it notes.

We settled on *Jeeves*, the name of the butler in the P. G. Wodehouse books she had read me. And Colton was right; it *did* feel good to use Jeeves. I had more independence. I could walk better, I stood steadier on my feet, and the ataxia would reduce as soon as I had Jeeves beside me. I tried to lean into the change, to lean with confidence, and Jeeves became known by name among our small circle of friends. He accompanied me everywhere, and to my surprise, I liked him more and more.

I didn't feel brave. Most days I felt ridiculous—twenty-two years old and walking through the front door with a mobility aid I had only seen used by great-grandparents and fashionable men with mustaches in the nineteenth century. But something sacred was buried in that quiet surrender. I had spent so long gripping the edge of "normal," trying not to let go, trying to hold up an image of strength that was shattering me. But not until I had laid that version of myself down—limping and stubborn, angry and defeated—could something softer begin to grow.

The cane didn't take anything from me. It gave me back some of what I had been losing in the name of pride: movement, dignity, freedom. Freedom to admit my own dependence—not on broomsticks and random objects around me, but on something intentional, *made* to be my support. I thought surrender would mean a shift of identity. Instead, it meant getting some of my old identity back again. Surrender was a way for *Sydney* to keep moving forward, one Jeeves-supported step at a time.

The first groups of soldiers were being sent off day by day. Colton's departure date changed three times, over a week apart. It made planning difficult, especially because we had to coordinate travel with my mom, who would be flying to Kansas to get me, as well as supply a solid date for when we'd be leaving our apartment.

We tried to make the most of the time we had together, but Colton worked long days as he prepped with his unit for deployment. I sat or lay down alone most of the time and spent my empty hours researching FND. I watched video after video, read study after study, scoured news articles, medical pages, websites, and personal blogs. I read everything I could find. Many of the superficial searches matched what the neurologist had told me: trauma, anxiety, physical manifestation of mental symptoms. But as I dug deeper into the more recent medical studies, I found that much of this information was outdated. My research convinced me I had FND, but the neurologist who diagnosed me had an old-school style of thinking. He had explained it *wrong*.

I couldn't understand yet how all the information fit, but I did cling to at least one small shred of evidence: The physical changes FND brought to the brain could be detected by an fMRI machine. FND changed something physical. Something *real*. Not all in my head. Not my fault.

Every time I found new information on FND, I shared it with Colton. I found the online summary of prognoses hopeful too; most websites said people with FND often recovered fully. I hung on to this hope with every fiber of my being. *If they can get better, maybe with the right treatment, I can too.*

Singing

The first time I lost my ability to speak—right before Colton's deployment—the episode lasted three days. I woke up from a seizure, and the words were gone. My tongue had no way of reaching them. The dark pool between my mind and mouth swirled deep and uncontrollable. Seventy-two hours is a long time when you're not sure if something will end.

I found it darkly ironic that after losing so much already, I would also lose my voice. We often say "there are no words" as a platitude, but in grief, it's a reality: No words are strong enough to carry the weight of some pain. Colton took it harder than I did. "I miss you," he said over and over, as if saying it might bring my voice back. It felt like a small death.

For three days, I lived in the tomb. The third day brought resurrection. Literally. Easter Sunday 2021.

Colton asked me if I still wanted to go to church. I shook my head. Without words, how could I? He smiled. "That's not a good enough reason."

I stood beside him for the first hymn, ready to mouth the words.

"Christ the Lord is risen today, Alleluia!"

By the end of the first line, I knew something strange was happening. If I stopped singing and tried to speak, the words got stuck in my mouth as they had done all morning. But singing felt different. I tried—timid, tentative. And suddenly, there it was: my voice, praising with the congregation.

"Love's redeeming work is done, Alleluia!"

My voice resurrected into praise of the resurrected Christ, singing triumphantly from my place of defeat with the church triumphant, the freedom of words flowing from a tongue formerly silenced.

We put our seal of sadness on the graves of our losses and bid them goodbye.

No words. Only pain inexpressible, full of sorrow.

But God says to our losses: "I will break the seal on your graves as I broke His. I have swallowed your sorrow whole. In its place, because Christ has risen, I have for you joy inexpressible, full of glory."

I tugged on Colton's sleeve and put my lips up to his ear. His voice choked. He stopped to listen. His strong voice silenced by emotion, my weak one exultant with praise.

"Death in vain forbids him rise, Alleluia!

"Christ has opened paradise, Alleluia!"[3]

One day, every silencing of our strength will fall away as we join the saints in worship. Every silence will give way to an unbroken song of glory. *This*, I thought, *is what singing feels like in heaven.*

Back home, Colton went out for groceries. I filled the quiet room with stammering syllables. When Colton came back, I rushed to the door, stuttering but exuberant: "I-IIIII c-c-caaaaan sssssss-speak!"

In our weakness, God meets us with His strength. These moments—small resurrections in broken places—are prisms refracting His beauty.

Colton bent down and kissed me. "I love you." He didn't have to say it. It was all there, in his eyes.

PART TWO

deployment

SEVEN

unbelief

Deployment, week three. School, week one: picture day.

Colton was in Poland with his unit. I was in Idaho at college. The August sun bore down as I stood outside in a packed crowd of students. My black school robes clung to me despite the intentional lightness of my dress underneath, heat making them feel heavier with every passing minute.

New Saint Andrews is a private liberal arts college on the western edge of the Idaho panhandle. Its methodology and school structure are based, in large part, on Oxford University in England—which means classical learning, rigorous academics . . . and the mandatory practice of upperclassmen wearing robes to school events and final exams. This was my first year as an upperclassman, and wearing a robe to school picture day felt like a privilege and an honor. It did, that is, until we left air-conditioning.

Organizing an entire school for a group photo takes time—and poor Jeeves wouldn't be able to hold me up much longer. I swayed, thankful that my dear friend from Korea, Jinha—or Jane, as she let us Americans call her—stood next to me.

A numbness swept over me, sharp and sudden, leaving an icy wave of nausea in its wake. My vision blurred in and out, darkening, returning, then slipping away and out of focus into shadow again.

I struggled to speak, and the words came out slurred and distant: "I think I'm going to pass out." Jane later told me I repeated it twice. I don't remember. My vision went black.

I heard a male classmate's startled voice: "Oh! *Whoaaaaaa!*" Then everything went silent and dark. My senses returned in the opposite progression of how they'd left me. First, sound: the crisp British accent of our beloved dean, Dr. Edwards, quite near to my head.

"She told me she has seizures," he was saying. "She said they're not serious. We just need to support her and wait them out."

A woman's voice came from near my feet. "Let's elevate her legs a bit," she said. "It might help her regain consciousness."

The dry grass trickled down my bare skin as my legs were lifted. I smelled sweat, felt the presence of a crowd pressing over me. I fought to open my eyes, but they remained clamped shut. Weak tremors passed through my shoulders and legs, growing stronger every minute. I started convulsing. *No. Not here. Not now. In front of everyone?* The seizure swept over me. I drifted in and out of awareness, conscious of the world around me, muffled and far away, while my body jerked and spasmed before it.

It seemed ages before the convulsing stilled. I opened my eyes. Dr. Edwards knelt beside me in the grass, looking down at me and supporting my shoulders. A ring of students stood packed around us, watching with nervousness and excitement. Something this interesting didn't usually happen on school picture day.

The lady at my feet smiled. "There we go," she said as my eyes fought for full, clear vision through lingering spasms and pain.

"Yep, she's all right then." Dr. Edwards smiled. "You can hear us now, Sydney? You're all right?" I nodded. He rose and gestured to the other students. "Give her some space, at least. Some air!"

The lady remained crouched, keeping my legs elevated. "I used to work as an EMT," she explained. "Lie still for a while. I timed your seizure. It lasted less than a minute, so don't worry." With a kind smile, she added, "One of the gentlest seizures I've ever seen. Very quiet."

Her cheerful, confident handling of the situation steadied me, even as the waves of embarrassment grew stronger with every passing second. A few of the students helped me to my feet and guided me to the side of the field.

The heat of embarrassment bore down on me like that August sun. Everyone had seen it—the collapse, the jerking, the helplessness. My body had betrayed me in the most public way possible, in front of people I'd be living beside for the next three years.

"Do you want me to take you home?" the woman asked. "You don't have to stay here."

"Yes, please," I said. I still felt shaky and sick and couldn't imagine the awkwardness of trying to make my way back into the crowd of students and posing again as if nothing had happened. Worse yet, my symptoms were intensifying by the minute. When episodes like this begin, they often keep going, giving me little to no time to recover between them. I knew that unless I removed myself from the noise and stress of the situation and allowed my body to rest in quiet, the cycle might continue unabated.

I had been wondering how it would go: returning with a disability to my small college. Everyone there had known me as a healthy and adventurous freshman just a year before. I didn't know any other young person with a cane. I didn't know how to warn my fellow classmates about my seizure episodes. I hadn't expected to tell them like *this*—or to include the entire faculty in the process.

Jane helped me to the car. "I caught you when you fainted," she said, concern for me etched in her face. Her Korean accent always sounded more prominent under stress. "But I'm so sorry. It's not that you're heavy, but I couldn't hold you very long. So I laid you on the grass."

I smiled. Jane stood shorter than I did. I would not have expected her to hold me while I sagged, a dead weight in the hot Idaho sun. The fact that she worried about offending me made me laugh a little despite myself.

"It's okay, Jane," I said, grinning. "You were so kind to catch me at all."

She looked at me anxiously. "Did I do the right thing?" she asked. "Did I help you the right way?"

In that moment, it dawned on me: No one else thought this was embarrassing. In fact, everyone was far more concerned about their own performance in the scene—anxious to have done enough, acted appropriately, helped in the right way.

I had been yearning for more connection—for a community who could understand, who knew what it was like to live with a diagnosis. I had begun to find such a community online by tentatively sharing my story. The support had come pouring in.

"This happens to me too!"

"Your cane is so beautiful!"

"Wow, I'm glad you shared this. Thanks for the encouragement."

A few weeks before, a far bigger online account than mine had sent me a private message. "Hey, would you be willing to share your story and a few photos with our audience?" they had asked. "We'd love to do a feature on you!"

I had chosen the Instagram handle *The Anne Girl*, not only because of my lifelong affinity for *Anne of Green Gables*, but also because I naively thought that if I used my middle name, no one who knew me personally would find the account and connect it to me. That delusion lasted about three weeks. The whole time, I had been imagining how sharing my story online might bring me closer to *that* community—the ones who could "really understand," but the whole time I had missed that right in front of me stood a flesh-and-blood friend who believed me, who caught me when I fainted, who—rather than hanging back out of awkwardness or embarrassment—stepped forward to offer support in my most vulnerable moments.

We all have what I call "Main Character Complex." We see ourselves as the main character in the story—not only in our own narratives but in everyone else's too. Then we have a moment—maybe we trip on the sidewalk and fall next to a garbage bin; or a well-meaning stranger calls 911 when they see us having a medical symptom we experience *all the time*; or our signature comes out looking like a second grader's due to hand tremors; or we spill someone's coffee because we can't feel their cup with our numb hand—and we think: *Wow, this is such an embarrassing moment for a main character to have.*

The truth is, everyone else is doing the same thing: seeing the moment through *their* lens, wondering if they played *their* role well enough. For them, I wasn't the main character but rather a supporting role in their own story: a chance for them to act with compassion or courage in the face of the day's plot twist.

As I remembered this, the weight of embarrassment began to lift—for the moment. The awkwardness I felt didn't match how others saw the situation. To them, my episode wasn't a spectacle but a call to action, a test or proof of their kindness and instinct. And more than anything, they needed reassurance that *they* had done the right thing.

This moment marked a turning point in how I saw my disability; if I wore the label of *embarrassment*, I had placed it on myself. No one had assigned it to me. My confidence reached a turning point at that realization: My feelings of shame only defined me in my own head.

I had noticed that using a cane in public as a young person garnered attention, sometimes negative. Whenever I felt someone staring at me, openly noticing my biggest insecurity, I wanted to shrink down and away—make myself small and invisible, avoid eye contact, and shuffle out of sight. But after my realization, I started forcing myself to react in opposition to how I felt. I made myself stand up straighter and walk with more confidence and poise. I made eye contact with observers and gave them a big and cheerful smile, keeping my head erect, my gait steady and certain. Something strange happened. The more I pretended to be confident, the more my feelings of confidence grew.

The story you're writing about your vulnerability may not be the story others are reading. What if the moments you dread the most—those raw, exposed moments where you feel helpless—are the very moments that invite others to step in, show kindness, become part of a picture bigger than themselves? What if your story is part of someone else's story, part of their sanctification, part of what God is using to shape them just as He is using this to shape you? What if those moments of "embarrassment" are actually invitations to be fully human?

I squeezed Jane's hand. "You did the right thing. Thank you for helping me. You were perfect."

The Ballroom

Deployment is the year pain danced. She danced like a pagan, like a hornet, like a ballerina in stilettos. She pirouetted across my skin, landing neat, stab-like. Pain danced—oh the irony!—on a body from which she had robbed that ability. I was her ballroom. She was the star.

When I think back to the deployment, I remember Pain. And Fear.

I seized in public bathrooms, against coffee shop windows, on wet sidewalks in the dark. Hallucinations dogged my steps. I fell almost every day, sometimes lying and convulsing for hours before regaining the strength to drag myself across the floor to the mattress. Using the bathroom was often a monumental feat—so monumental that I would go a day without food or drink if I didn't know if I'd be able to crawl across the room to get there. My weight dropped like crumbs from the kitchen counter. I called 911 twice for myself, after hours of lying on the floor in terrified exhaustion.

The first week landed me in the emergency room twice—first for a cerebrospinal-fluid leak and then for fear the blood patch to repair it had been dislodged.

"I have family members calling me," Colton said over the phone, "telling me I should make you drop out of school and go stay with your family in Washington while I'm gone."

One of the hardest things about chronic illness is being forced to juxtapose *safety* against almost everything else you love. *Safety* becomes *X*. And everything else in your life is a math equation. College? Well, can you safely get across a campus? Coffee shop with a friend? What if you have a seizure over your caramel macchiato? You want to hold a baby, take a shower by yourself, drive your car, stand during worship at church, make your own meals, go to the doctor alone, or sit through a movie? Think through it, ma'am . . . algebraically.

"What did you say to them?" I asked, turning my thoughts back to Colton on the phone. "Do you think I should drop out and go home?"

"I think it's your choice."

I shook my head. *I only have bad options*, I thought. I could go back to Kansas, to live alone where we had been stationed and where I barely knew anyone. I could go home and live with my parents like a kid again, with nothing to focus my mind or make me feel purposeful despite this pain. Or I could stick with the plan of staying in school, where at least I had something to do—if I could just get through it.

"I want to keep going," I said. "I think this is the best option I have."

The line fell quiet for a moment. "I think so too."

The words didn't make me feel better. My stomach clenched with anxiety.

Nine months, I thought, staring at the ceiling. *Nine months. And this is just week one.*

People often tell me my disability is the antagonist of my story, and I am the hero—rising in courage to overcome my suffering. But that's not how I see it. The true antagonist in my story isn't my body. It's the despair that clutches my heart, that makes me want to sink into my own brokenness—separate from God, belly-up, on the vinyl apartment floor on which I've fallen. And the hero isn't me; it's Jesus. The One who died and rose to overcome all. Who crushed the serpent on its belly, by rising victorious over poverty and pain, sin and sorrow, despair and death.

I'm not the main character. I'm not the great overcomer. I'm the pot. Handle-less, remember? The clay in the hands of the Potter. A few words in the story He is writing for His own glory. And even when I can't make sense of the plot or feel the arc of redemption, it is enough—more than enough—to know I'm held within it.

How would you live if you were guaranteed a happy ending? Do that.

Fear whispers that I will always be this way. Early on, I shut out the thought, buried it far away, deep inside, where it couldn't touch me. Such a thought could be self-fulfilling, couldn't it? Such a thought could alter my prognosis. Didn't I have to *believe* I'd get better to get better?

That's what Google said: Patients who are confident in the treatment process have the highest rates of recovery from FND. I sat on waiting lists for cognitive behavioral therapy, eye movement desensitization and reprocessing (EMDR) treatment, and physical therapy. Those options were still a few months out. In the meantime, I tried to believe so hard it stung my insides.

"Are you safe in bed?" Colton would ask on the phone—first question every night.

"Yes."

"Have you eaten or drunk anything today?"

"Not yet."

"Why?!"

"Because I won't be able to get to the bathroom."

"Drink water!" Colton would say over the phone. "Just go in your bed and change your sheets when you feel better."

This is already degrading enough, I thought. Falling every day. Getting stuck on the floor for hours. Shimmying on my stomach onto my mattress. Crawling on paralyzed elbows and knees to the toilet or kitchen. Sitting on the cold enamel of the bathtub to bathe. Did I really want to add bed-wetting to the list? No. I'd rather be thirsty.

We often talk about how those before the time of Jesus died looking forward to the promise—the promise that a Savior would arrive and redeem them from their sin (Hebrews 11). That is true. But what is also true is that we *still* die looking forward to the promises. Christ died and rose again, not as the ultimate *fulfillment* of the promise, but as the ultimate *purchase* of the ultimate fulfillment of the promise.

When He died, He said: "It is finished."

And when He rose, God said: "It is finished indeed."

We not only die looking forward to the promises, but we also die *every day* looking forward to the promises. For us, there is not only hope; there is confidence. For if in Christ we die, in Christ we will rise again.

Sunflowers

Sunflowers are my favorite. I think they're testaments to hope in suffering.

In Kansas, before Colton's deployment, we once stumbled upon a tiny cluster of wild sunflowers growing on the side of the freeway. They were tall and gangly, only slightly larger than wild daisies, but their yellow heads shot up along the roadside, looking straight into the hot Kansas sun. Colton pulled off without saying a word, got out of the car, and gathered some. I smiled. He always did that for me, every time we passed a flower. No matter how small the flower, his brand-new-husband radar was raised and ready—he never missed one.

Even when battered by wind and heat, sunflowers instinctively turn their faces toward the sun. When the Kansas sky clouds over in a sheet of pale gray, the sunflower *still* turns. What is she following? When she can't see the sun, the sunflower acts faithfully; the sunflower acts as if she *does* see the sun. And before long, within hours, within days, her faithfulness is rewarded. The sun appears from behind the pale, insignificant clouds, and the sunflower rejoices that she wasted no time in searching for light, for her head is already turned toward it.

Tilt with me now—just an inch—toward where the sun should be. Kansas cloud cover be darned.

EIGHT

burden

She sat at the table on the other side of two cups of tea. With bright eyes and shoulder-length graying hair, her presence saturated the kitchen-dining room, filled with so many plants I felt like we were having a tea party in a tropical rainforest. Her parrot was perched on the back of the seat next to her, preening its feathers. Every so often, it cocked its head to glare at me with a bitter expression—something Mrs. Leidenfrost explained stemmed from my black hair, a color the bird apparently detested.

"Be nice," the parrot croaked, its eyes beaded in my direction.

It was a few months into Colton's deployment, and the time had come for his first overseas drill. While one might think it wouldn't make much difference whether Colton was five thousand miles away in Poland or in Germany, it meant our phone calls and sporadic texts were dialed down to radio silence for several weeks. It meant the days I couldn't get out of bed were spent in complete isolation, without even a human voice to break the silence. It meant my primary source of human understanding and comfort had been taken from me. I always dreaded drill weeks, and this one, over winter break, meant I had nothing to break up the loneliness of the days when I wasn't feeling well enough to get out or socialize. My ongoing depression had sunk in deep, and I confided my struggle to one of the school faculty, also an elder at the local church.

"I'm not sure how to deal with this," he had said, "but I know someone who does."

And that's how I came to be sitting with Mrs. Leidenfrost—missionary to the Bakwé people, wife to a man translating the Bible into a language never written before, chronic illness sufferer, and now a voice of hope and encouragement to hundreds of local women walking through suffering themselves. Mrs. Leidenfrost smiled and turned her attention to the legal pad in front of her. "This," she said, drawing a small circle, "is your pain. Right now, it's all you can see." I stared at the circle, the bubble on a legal pad that represented all my struggle in life. There was something hopeless in the way it sat there, closed off, no opening, no escape. There was no other circle inside it.

Sometimes it feels as if pain is the whole story from beginning to end, as if nothing else fits. A circle as a shape, after all, doesn't invite interruption. It *is* the whole story—from the global scale downward to the tiny period at the end of this sentence. And what if your circle sucks? What if you feel like you got a lousy artist? Are you stuck then? In a cycle that doesn't break?

Mrs. Leidenfrost drew a second, larger circle around the first. "But this," she continued—oh, thank the Lord for the *buts* in His story!—"this represents the people God is blessing through your pain." Her pencil glided, each new circle growing larger until it reached the edges of the page. "As you endure this, as you continue to look to God, the blessing will ripple outward—further and further. The people you bless will bless others, and so on."

She tapped the outermost circle with her pencil. "You'll never fully know, in this life, how far those blessings will reach. But know this: God is blessing many people through your pain. He is working. You must trust that He is."

I wanted to believe her. I wanted to imagine my suffering rippling outward in unseen ways—that my smile in the emergency room echoed upward into a halo around my head, and when I cheerfully answered Colton's phone call from the middle of my apartment floor, an invisible Harry Potter sorting hat muttered and mused, wondering if he should name my abundant courage or saintly kindness as the most prominent of my traits.

But instead of ripples, my mind filled with images—stock portraits of pleasant, patient, pitiful sufferers. Beth from *Little Women*, lying on the beach with sea breezes blowing color into her pale cheeks, whispering about her life slipping out like the tide, and not being afraid of dying, except for the possibility of being homesick even in heaven. I always wanted to like Beth. She was so good. So sweet. So completely . . . unrelatable.

Tiny Tim from *A Christmas Carol* was cute until I got a crutch of my own. Then I realized the gaping hole in Dickens's storytelling: Crutches are not halos for people. A cough isn't cute, and a limp doesn't provide a likability bonus. Suffering doesn't sprinkle one with sainthood, and dying isn't darling. Not like that.

Does God only use Beths and Tiny Tims? Or does He use closet Scrooges too? To put it in biblical terms, do we dare to see that the God who used a small shepherd boy to slay a giant also worked through him as an adult king who had affairs, murdered honorable men, practiced polygamy, lost two children as a result of his terrible sins, and had hands so bloody they couldn't build the temple? I looked at Lisa Leidenfrost. "How do you *know* when God is using your pain to bless others?"

She met my gaze. "That's not your burden to carry," she said. "It is God's. It is not your job to bless others through your pain; that's far too big a task for you. Your only responsibility is to look to God in your suffering and remain faithful. As you do, He will work through you for His glory. You may never know how—and you don't *need* to know. It is enough to know Him."

She drew her pencil to the bottom of the paper and sketched a small stick figure with a horizontal line two inches above its head. "This person," she said, pointing to the figure, "has strength. The limits of their strength don't even touch them." Then she drew two more figures, each with the line inching closer to their heads. Finally, she sketched a tiny stick figure with the line resting right on top of it. "This is you," she said, smiling gently. "You feel weak because your limits are pressing down on you. But you *are* blessed, because that is where God wants you to be. Here, He can give you His strength as your own. When you are weak, He is strong."

Above the figure, she wrote "God's Strength" and drew an arrow straight through the top of the paper. "You were never meant to carry this alone. But God's strength is infinite, and because of your weakness, you'll experience it in a way most people never will. It *is* a gift. Truly."

The limits of your strength might feel so close to you that you can feel it crushing your rib cage. But the crushing place—the crucible, the awful ending of your own feeble power—is exactly where God plans to fill you with His.

She leaned back, her voice quieter. "When they diagnosed my daughter with multiple sclerosis, she went through a period of grief over the life she felt God had robbed of her. One day, I asked her, 'If you had a choice—if you could live your ideal life and accomplish everything you wanted and feel happy and successful and live a long time *and do nothing great for the kingdom of God*, or you could choose the suffering and pain and affliction God has given you, *knowing He will use it to His great and eternal glory*—which one would you pick?'"

Her daughter had answered without hesitation, "The second one."

"That is what God picked for you also."

She pulled out another yellow sheet from the legal pad and looked at me. "You are carrying more burdens than you're supposed to," she said, making a series of lines stacked on top of each other in list form. "The Bible makes it very simple: The burdens you can't control aren't the ones you're supposed to carry. Now, what are things you can't control?"

I started listing items off the top of my head: my health and physical limitations, my safety, the separation from Colton, my past.

"Yes," she interrupted quietly, "your past. That includes your regrets and your guilt. You can no longer control the past, and therefore, it is not a burden you are meant to carry."

She looked at me. "You don't understand the grace of God."

I stared at her. As a pastor's kid, raised in a Christian home, I couldn't remember a time when I did not love Jesus. Well-versed in Scripture, theology, and doctrine—how could I not understand the grace of God? Wasn't that, well . . . pretty basic?

"You don't," she said, seeing my expression. "You see, even if everything that has happened was entirely your fault—even," she said, "if you had committed the greatest of possible sins—because of Jesus, you would still be forgiven and covered by the blood of Christ. You would still have no burden to carry. No guilt to bear. How much more so when none of this was ever in your hands to begin with?"

I understood then: You can try to carry guilt as your penance. You can let it devour you, eat you whole, and make you feel like a martyr. Martyrdom feels holy, it feels atoning, it feels redemptive. But holding on to guilt doesn't make one a martyr. Guilt makes a criminal. The only Martyr who can die for someone else's guilt already did, two thousand years ago, on a cross in Golgotha. His death took your guilt away. His resurrection made you clean. Carrying guilt in penance doesn't make you holy; it undermines the full redemption of the only holiness that has ever been given to you. You cannot atone for what Jesus already covered. You can only receive it. Like grace.

Mrs. Leidenfrost went back to the list on the yellow pad and said, "I will add three more burdens you're not meant to carry: the future, your sanctification, and other people. You can't control any of these. These are God's burdens—and He *wants* to carry them. He is very jealous, you know. He will not make it easy for you to put yourself up in His place, to carry the burdens He is supposed to bear. He will make it difficult, crushingly difficult, because He wants you to give them back to Him and have Him bear them for you. Trying to do otherwise sets you up for being struck twice: once with the trial, and again when you will accept no help. Of course this illness is crushing you. It is above your strength—above any human strength. But it is not above God's strength. Why carry for so long what He can carry easily?"

One afternoon before the deployment, Colton and I were lying on the bed, shoulder to shoulder, talking. He stretched out his hand toward me, and I took it with both of mine, holding it tightly against my chest like a prize. He tugged, pretending to pull it back, and I wrestled with him, gripping with all my strength to keep it on my side of the bed.

His hand began to quake. "Oh, no! I'm shaking!" he said with mock alarm.

"Maybe it's because you're straining," I teased, bracing harder and holding tighter, proud of myself for putting up such a good fight.

Colton laughed. "Straining?"

Then, without shifting his grip or lifting a single finger more in effort, he pulled his hand—and my entire body with it—across the bed toward him.

As I felt my body slide across the mattress, easily, effortlessly, I started laughing too. I had been using 100 percent of my strength to keep Colton's hand close. Straining. Bracing. Giving it my all. But when that man dragged my whole body across the bed, I realized he had been using, like, 10 percent of his strength to play back.

My body feels so heavy sometimes I have to work just to hold it upright. Because it's so heavy, I hesitate to ask for help. How could I ask anyone to lift this deadweight—this sack of bones, tendons, ligaments, and pain—when I can barely lift my head up from my chest? But then Colton lifts me, and I feel my own heaviness dissipate right into his steady arms. What is hard for me is not hard for him. What is too great for my strength is not too great for his.

We keep clenching burdens to our chests, straining with every ounce of effort, proud of how tightly we can hold on. But we forget that God is not straining. He is not trembling. He does not need to brace Himself. He waits for you to let go, so He can draw you close. What is too great for your strength is not too great for His.

Mrs. Leidenfrost drew an arrow upward. "Your job is simple: Look to Him. This is God's will for you: 'Rejoice always, pray without ceasing, in everything give thanks.'[1] Just look and look and give and give. That is all you are called to do—and even in this, He will help you."

She drew more arrows from stick-figure me up to the top of the page. "Right now, you're telling God who you are instead of letting Him tell you. Speak back to the voices that come at you from the outside. Tell them they are wrong. Tell them the truth of who you are in Christ. *Respond.* That is part of the fight. That is part of believing what God says is true about who you are in Him."

Tears blurred my vision. "I feel like if I trusted God enough," I whispered, "this wouldn't feel so hard. A few weeks before my brother Isaiah died, I prayed this thing I almost wish I hadn't prayed. I felt far from God, really hardened and distant. I prayed in my car one day that God would break me, because I felt that was the only way I could learn to trust Him. But . . ." I said. "But it feels like He keeps breaking me over and over, as if He's saying with each new blow, 'I did not break you enough the last time. You did not learn as much as you were supposed to, so I must break you again.'"

To my surprise, Mrs. Leidenfrost smiled. "Don't you see that even in that prayer, you were trying to control your sanctification—telling God how to work in your life? You feel as though you overstepped your bounds—that you didn't know what you were asking for—and now you're reaping the consequences of your mistake. God doesn't give you control over your sanctification. He just asks you to look to Him in faith and obedience, and *He* will sanctify you. You weren't in control of that. You were trying to be God."

God, let me help You with my holiness. How many times do we pray that prayer? *This is the plan: I trust You, so You bless me.* How often do we imagine ourselves bravely bearing a certain kind of suffering, only to be knocked flat by a trial we could have never foreseen? *No, not this one, God. Anything but this.* We are sucked in, pulled down, wondering at which point we lost control of the life we never controlled to begin with. *God, I didn't expect trusting You to feel so much like loss. I didn't expect faith to feel like drowning. It feels like one of us screwed up big-time . . . and sometimes, I don't think it was me.* God seldom gives us the trials we've prepared for.

Mrs. Leidenfrost's voice grew soft. "Say *amen* to God now, at the beginning of the trial," she said. "That is faith. To say *amen* at the end, when you can see clearly, is not faith. Faith does not see clearly. Trust God now, and He will bless you and grow your faithfulness."

The most terrifying prayer you ever pray might begin with the word *amen.*

She walked back with me through the snow. She gave me some assignments to do, and advice for how to cope with things once I got home. I showed her what my walk looked like with a cane—I had never shown anyone else in Moscow. I don't know why I did it, but it felt safe.

These are my limits, my vulnerabilities, my embarrassments.

I know you have yours.

Show them to a Mrs. Leidenfrost. And show them to God.

As we parted, she handed me her two books and her yellow sheets of notes, lingering like her words, little flames amid the snow.

NINE

belief

I went into the seizure—long, violent—and woke up unable to move. It had happened before, many times, but this time felt different. No matter what I tried, I could not recover. Stuck on the mattress on the floor, I struggled, alone in my own thoughts. I didn't know why at the time, what triggered the flashbacks—pain or confusion. I wanted to cover my eyes with my hands, block out the images, the hallucinations, the memories, but I couldn't move my arms.

Every attempt to move sent a fresh wave of panic surging through me. The feeling of being trapped rose up in my chest, strangling me, triggering the thoughts, the memories, the terror. I shoved the voice down and kept trying to stay calm. If I could just move my arms, maybe I could drag myself across the floor to the kitchen and get some water—it would help ground me, and anyway, I was parched with thirst.

I lay in bed another seven hours before I could move my arms. I laboriously rolled myself off the mattress, hit the floor with a thud, and started pulling my way across with my elbows. I brought my phone with me, knowing I should have a way to reach help if I needed to, but it made movement cumbersome. At first, I tried to crawl with it in my hand, but the phone felt too heavy, too unwieldy. Eventually, I resorted to pushing it a few feet ahead of me, dragging myself toward it, then pushing it forward again.

Slide phone a few feet ahead. Plant elbows. Drag to phone. Head down. Breathe. Slide phone a few feet ahead . . .

Every second of dragging sapped more energy out of me. I hadn't eaten or drunk for almost nine hours. My body weakened and my throat screamed with thirst. *I just have to get to the kitchen,* I thought, but I never made it that far.

Halfway across the room, my arms began locking up again. Every attempt to move triggered violent spasms inward, excruciating tightening of my muscles, spastisized, shaking uncontrollably. My elbows would jerk back toward my torso, skidding violently against the hardwood floor. It made it impossible to pull myself forward. I tried to relax the convulsive movements of my limbs and body. My head kept slamming against the ground. I could feel a knot forming. *Just stop. Just relax. Try to roll over and protect your head.* After a few minutes and a vast amount of effort, I pushed partly over onto my side. I lay there panting, trying to breathe, trying to make the convulsions slow and pass through me until my muscles could relax against some of the pain.

Only humans are proud enough to fume against God while lying face down on the floor in their tiny apartment. And I fumed. I fumed against the deployment, the seizure, and the fall. I fumed against the floor and the indignity of my position. I fumed no one was there to help me. I fumed that I had undone my shred of progress. I fumed there was only a shred of progress to undo.

The thought, so easy—*I am just the sort of person this thing happens to. I am the great progress-unwinder. I can never catch a break. I hate my life.*

Shame and self-loathing feel like humility, but self-flagellation is always an act of pride. We carry, rather than surrender, everything outside of our control. Like Sisyphus, we curse ourselves to carry our own burdens up the mountain alone. Like Satan, we find it better to reign in hell than to serve in heaven. We write, *I am the worst* and slap it on the wall—framed, and in calligraphy.

My phone showed 11:00 p.m. Somewhere in Poland, Colton would wake up soon. If I could just text him, he could help me think through what to do. My own mind slogged with heaviness, and the longer I waited, the more I wasted precious time and strength.

Careful not to move my arm, careful not to shift a single unnecessary muscle, I lifted a finger from the floor and planted it heavily on my phone screen. It lit up. I dragged my finger up and across. The movement triggered the convulsions again and I tried to work through them just enough to type the password. By the time I finished, I had to wait again. The effort had left me spent.

Don't let the phone lock again. Keep it awake. I lifted my finger jerkily, set it down, lifted it again, repeating the motion just enough to keep the screen from going dark. Weakness crept over me with numbing tendrils. *Soon, I may not be able to move at all.*

Slowly, painstakingly, I dragged my finger over the letters, trying to breathe through the convulsions it caused. I did my best, but the few words I got through were barely coherent. I prayed it would be enough—that he would see it—and that he would know.

Thirty minutes later, my phone pinged.

The screen lit up, Colton's name glowing in the darkness. The phone vibrated—he was calling. With a massive effort, I threw my arm forward and dragged my finger across the screen. I could hear Colton's muffled voice on the other end of the line, trying to speak to me. I couldn't speak right away, but I hoped he could hear me gasping. I hoped it would tell him to stay on the line with me. I worried he would think he hadn't reached me, hang up, and try again, which would start the whole process over.

"Sydney? Sydney?" his voice filled the empty room. I wanted to cry with gratitude. His voice. He called. He came to me. Five thousand miles away perhaps, but someone *knew*.

"C-Colton?" I gasped out, barely above a whisper. My torso spasmed again, catching my breath.

"C-Colton, I—" my voice broke under the effort. *Stop jerking*, I told myself angrily. *Just get the words out.*

"Sydney? Are you okay? Do you need help?"

"Y-yes," I gasped. "H-hold on."

I stayed quiet a few minutes, willing my body to relax, trying to get the spasms to stop. If I could only keep myself still, try to talk without moving any other part of me, maybe it would be enough to get the words out.

Colton waited, patient, his voice gentle and calm. "Take your time."

My head was still smashed against the floor, cheek pressed against the cold wood. I opened my mouth, slowly, careful not to move my head, no other part of my body, and my lips no more than necessary. The severe dehydration had left me without a voice, and I carefully croaked the words out to him, in a slow, hoarse whisper.

"I fell. I can't move," I breathed. "Door . . . is locked. Can't . . . get help."

"How long have you been like this?"

I struggled to count. Bed. Crawling. Floor. How long?

"Ele-ven hours," I whispered.

A brief pause.

"Okay." His voice quieted. I stopped trying to think. Too much energy. I simply waited for him to answer.

"Sydney, listen." His voice came over the line again, firm, decisive. "You need to call 911."

My heart sank. I had called 911 once during a similar episode. The emergency room doctors had taken one look at the records containing my diagnosis and stopped believing me. The experience had been long, shameful, and excruciating.

"P-please, no."

"Babe, you have to."

My body convulsed again. I tried to speak through the gasps of pain. "They won't believe me."

"They don't need to believe you," Colton said firmly. "You need help getting off the floor. You need to be hydrated again. You need to be in a safe place so the pain can go down and you can eat something and regain strength. They can do that."

I didn't answer.

"You're not in danger because of the paralysis, Sydney. You're in danger because you can't get to anything on your own. It's only going to get worse the longer you lie there. I'm going to hang up. Call 911. Then call me right back as soon as you're able to. Call them now, Sydney. Okay?"

"Okay."

The line went silent.

It took forever to dial. Still longer to explain.

"Okay, ma'am. And why can't you get up?"

Why? Why? I don't know why. I don't know why my body is like this. I don't understand this stupid disease. No one does. How am I going to explain to you something I don't understand myself?

Keys rattled. The door swung open.

"Ma'am? Ma'am, can you hear us?"

I tried to answer. My eyes were heavy. Through tiny, weighted slits I could see shadows moving above my head. I heard the tramp of heavy boots on the floor. Hands gripped my arms, my ankles.

"One, two, three, *lift*."

My body lowered onto something soft and . . . fuzzy? *My blanket?* I thought confusedly. *My blanket from my bed . . .*

The blanket tightened around me as my body lifted, heavy, sagging down in the center. Boots tramped forward. I moved backward, headfirst, toward what must have been the doorway. I heard the elevator open.

"She's fading. She's fading!"

A rough finger raked down my sternum. My body gave one small spasm, then lay still.

"Her breathing's low! Her breathing's low!"

Knuckles raked across my chest again.

"Sydney! Sydney! Stay with us!"

Blackness swept over me, and in the blackness, a memory. Not my name. Not my name they were calling. They were calling for Isaiah. And I was losing him, I was losing him.

And then he was gone.

When you have a rare illness, you're like a puzzle bought at a thrift store. No one really likes to get their puzzles at the thrift store. Everyone knows it's a bad idea. So when someone finally does pick you up and take you home, you're full of hope: Finally, someone believes they can solve me. Someone believes I have all my pieces!

They start putting you together and you feel your confidence rising piece by piece. Wow, four corners! That's gotta mean something, right? Surely that's a good sign! You watch the colors come into place, forming shapes. You may not be as pretty as other puzzles, but by gosh you'll settle for just being solved!

You're almost done. Just a few pieces left. But they don't seem to fit anywhere. The piece-to-empty-space ratio doesn't seem quite right. "Please don't give up on me," you whisper. "You've come so far! It's the job! It's why you bought the puzzle, right? For the challenge? Push through. Complete the picture. Solve me, please." But the longer the person sits there looking at the picture that no longer makes sense, the less you start doubting their puzzle-solving abilities and the more you start doubting your ability to be solved.

You sense the frustration long before they say it: "That's what I get for buying a puzzle from the thrift store."

Your pieces are unceremoniously scraped across the dining room table and back into the box, a little bent at the edges from wear and tear. You're not brand-new after all. This isn't the first person who's tried to solve you. You're thrown up on the shelf. Then you collect dust.

"Oh, don't grab that puzzle, little Johnny! It's missing some pieces."

After a while you start to believe them. Not everyone can be this bad at solving puzzles. Maybe you *are* missing pieces after all. Maybe you truly *are* unsolvable.

Most doctors are paid by the patient, not by the piece.

In the ER, I forced my voice to be as calm and steady as possible as I recounted what had happened. I avoided any sign of fear or anxiety, knowing they would immediately assume my symptoms were stress-induced. I made no desperate pleas for help, no frantic suggestions to search into what went wrong. I calmly explained that I had called 911 because I lived alone and the flare-up had left me stranded and incapable of recovering by myself. If I could get some fluids, eat something, and someone helped regain movement in my arms and legs, I knew I'd be fine to go home.

The doctor on call saw me long enough to say one sentence: "When we got the call, I thought it was you." I didn't see him again.

They started me on a saline drip, but no food yet. I lay on the bed for hours, and then the nurse entered abruptly.

"The saline's done so I'm unhooking you. You can go home," she said, beginning to remove the IV from my arm.

I stared at her. "But—I still can't walk."

"I think you can now." An edge of sarcasm sliced her voice. "Didn't you say you were only dehydrated?"

I took a slow breath. "No," I began carefully. "I said I became dehydrated because of the *paralysis*—I couldn't get water on my own. I feel stronger now, but I still can't move my legs." I gestured to where they lay, bent, cold, and twisted on the hospital bed. "I just need a little help to be able to walk again. It should only take a few minutes."

"Our physical therapist isn't on call this time of night," she said.

"I don't need a physical therapist. I do this on my own all the time. Tonight was just worse than usual." I kept my voice even. "Anyone could help me. My husband does it too—I just need a little support while I regain movement."

She nodded. "I'll talk to the doctor."

"Thank you," I said. "Also . . . is there any chance I could get assistance to the restroom?" The saline solution had done its job, and I needed to go.

"Sure," she said curtly, and left.

Thirty minutes later, another nurse arrived.

"We need to insert a catheter?" she said, holding out a paperwork form to me. "Please sign here."

It's like a bad movie. I looked at her, confused. "I don't . . . need a catheter," I said slowly. "I just need assistance to the restroom. I can use the restroom on my own if someone helps me get there."

"Oh. Is that because you can walk now?"

I looked at her. *Is she baiting me? Baiting me to do what?* I began again. "No . . . I still can't walk . . ." I said. "But if someone could just help support me as I try to regain movement, I think I could walk again very soon."

"I see. So, you still can't walk."

"Yes."

"And you need the restroom."

"Yes."

"So how do you propose we get you there?"

I looked at her, amazed. "Do . . . do you guys have, um . . . a wheelchair?"

She didn't answer, just tapped her foot, eyes locked on mine, eyebrow raised just a hair.

"You see why inserting the catheter is necessary," she continued, as if I hadn't said anything. "You can't walk to the bathroom, and you need to relieve yourself, so until you can walk there's just nothing else we can do to help you." She held out the form to me impatiently. "Please sign here. There are risks involved in inserting a catheter. And . . . it *will* hurt."

"Um . . . okay." I took the pen she offered me in a daze. "I don't really understand why it's necessary. This is the only way for me to use a bathroom?"

"Until you can walk," she said again, taking back the signed form. "Someone will be in shortly to insert the catheter."

I thought of how acting confident—despite my contrary feelings in the moment—led to true confidence. *Does it work for happiness too?* I wondered. I had once read a line from Joni Eareckson Tada, who said that every morning she prays God will give her His smile—because in the hardest moments of her day, she does not have one of her own.[1]

I closed my eyes and silently prayed the only prayer I could manage: *Lord, please give me Your smile tonight. Right now. In this hospital. Lord, I need Your smile.*

When the catheter nurse came in, I explained the situation to her.

"I didn't know you could use the bathroom with assistance," she said, looking surprised. "This procedure hardly seems necessary." I smiled as cheerfully as I could and thanked the Lord for the one person who had made sense to me since entering that hospital room.

The first nurse entered again, clearly annoyed. "And how will you get to a bathroom if you can't walk?" she asked again.

"Do you have a wheelchair?"

"I can try to find one," she said, as if wheelchairs were a scarce commodity in the empty ER room. "I'll go look."

She returned a few minutes later. "Get on. I'll take you myself."

"Thank you." With effort, I used my hands to push off the side of the hospital bed. I grimaced, my torso spasming as I supported myself with my arms and let myself fall into the wheelchair. The nurse stood watching me. She did not offer to help.

"Now, we're going to take you to the bathroom," she said loudly. I felt my face turning red. People were turning to stare at us. We were on our way to the bathroom just as I wanted, and I still felt helpless.

Life shoves you center stage, and it doesn't wait for you to learn your lines first. It doesn't give you Alexander the Great–esque courage before a persnickety nurse grabs the handles of your wheelchair. It doesn't hand you the lyrics about bright copper kettles and warm woolen mittens when you are faced with your *own* seven children scared of a thunderstorm. When your toddler launches across your bed at six in the morning, they don't wait for the days you're wide awake and yearning for chaos and elbow jabs with your morning coffee. When you make the cold, hard decision to keep living after a loss that knocks the air out of your lungs, it is almost never a post–Grand Canyon moment that makes you happy to be alive again. In fact, it is almost always the morning after the bone-crushing bludgeon that you are asked to get out of bed and carry on the business of living.

"All right, here we are," the nurse said, stopping the wheelchair in the middle of the open doorway. "Do you need help onto the toilet too?"

I eyed the six feet of daunting floor space before me and nodded. "That would be great, please. Thank you."

She lowered the brakes and came around to get me. She left the door wide open.

My mind blurred. Anxiety likes to whisper that you're an impostor; other people have it worse, after all. How dare you use a wheelchair if you can walk? Grief cries that your whole life will be as pain-filled and miserable as it is in this moment. Loss says, "God takes away and never gives." Pain tempts you to pull up the covers, face the wall, and shut out the world. Fear says, "Enough. You've had it. You can't face much more of this."

She grabbed my arm and I braced myself against the bathroom counter, slowly lowering onto the toilet seat. She stood over me, arms crossed, watching.

I didn't think they watched you go, I thought, trying to avoid eye contact. I could see her glaring down at me.

It's so much easier to follow along—the dog walking the master. You have to teach your feelings to heel. Confidence follows the erect head, direct eyes, and smile. Motivation to work out often comes after you start, not before. *Feelings* of kindness bloom after you act kindly. Gratitude follows the practice of giving thanks. Peace grows from living as if you already have it. So often, we wait for the right feeling to give us permission or incentive to move forward, but the real breakthrough comes when we stop waiting and start doing.

"Um . . . is it okay if you turn around, please? Sorry," I added.

She turned around without a word, back to me, arms still folded across her chest. Door still wide open.

The Smile Is Enough

In the early hours of the morning, I sat outside the emergency room entrance, shivering in my thin nightgown in the hospital wheelchair. I had finally gotten something to eat—a Nature Valley granola bar. Almost twenty-four hours had passed since my last meal.

I looked at my watch. Three a.m. The taxi would be here any minute.

Smile. Just smile. That was all just standard patient care, right?

As a teenager, I stumbled upon this gem of a C. S. Lewis quote in *Mere Christianity*: "Do not waste time bothering whether you 'love' your neighbor; act as if you did. As soon as we do this we find one of the great secrets. When you are behaving as if you loved someone, you will presently come to love him."[2]

At the time I discovered this quote, I was nannying for two rambunctious and rather difficult children under the age of four. Each shift was a ten-hour day, and often longer. I scrawled the words, "Act as if you did," in big block letters across the inside of my arm. It became my daily reminder to love those children with my actions, even when my feelings weren't there. *Act as if you did.* Act as if you love them, and the feelings will follow. Those words have stayed with me through depression, grief, disability, ingratitude, regret, unkindness, betrayal, abandonment, pain, and insecurity. They work as a compass pointing north when I am lost in the weeds of my feelings and self-doubt. *Act as if you did.* Act as if you love. Act as if you are happy. Act as if you are grateful. Act as if you are confident. Act as if you have joy. Act faithfully, and the feelings will follow.

I breathed out slowly, watching my breath come out in a fog. I looked down at the discharge papers. The diagnosis: "Anxiety attack and psychosomatic symptoms due to stress of husband being deployed to Afghanistan."

Anxiety attack? Afghanistan? Had they even listened to me?

Sometimes, the pain doesn't get a name that fits. Sometimes, the label you're handed feels more like an insult than a diagnosis. Lewis is not telling you to be fake or conceal your feelings under a mask to please those around you. The reminder is not to act *artificially* but to act *faithfully*. You don't make it through the slough of despond by denying the existence of sloughs (or despondency). You simply trust that as you take the next obedient step, God will meet you there—holding you, loving you, shaping you, and working through each small, seemingly insignificant, faithful moment where you choose to do the right thing.

At one point, lying in the hospital bed, I had felt myself going into a seizure and panicked. My mind was incoherent, frightened. I couldn't speak. I couldn't breathe. I looked wildly around for help. Two nurses were talking outside my room. I waved to them, gasping for air, terrified. They paused, looked directly at me, glanced at each other, then turned their backs and kept talking. The last thing I saw before going under was their smiles.

I used to think being misunderstood, mislabeled, or dismissed undermined the validity of my illness. Now, I believe certain kinds of real suffering bring neglect with them into the picture of pain. From Old Testament Job to the Incarnate Jesus, tragedy is often accompanied by those who blame the blameless for their trials. Luke, the physician, wrote about just such a person in that Gospel. "Now a woman, having a flow of blood for twelve years, who had spent all her livelihood on physicians and could not be healed by any, came from behind and touched the border of His [Jesus'] garment. And immediately her flow of blood stopped" (Luke 8:43–44).

Being unknowing and unknown was part of this woman's sorrow, and it was part of the invitation for redemption. It is part of what made her faith so glorious: "But Jesus said, 'Somebody touched Me, for I perceived power going out from Me.' Now when the woman saw that she was not hidden, she came trembling; and falling down before Him, she declared to Him in the presence of all the people the reason she had touched Him and how she was healed immediately. And he said to her, 'Daughter, be of good cheer; your faith has made you well. Go in peace'" (Luke 8:46–48).

At the time of this writing, I am four years into disability, and I have little hope of a cure. But after twelve years, this woman knew that all she needed was to touch Jesus' robe. The misunderstanding, the ostracization, the years of no answers did not show a lack of faith but became the vessel for its abundance. Redemption does not merely work backward in time to heal corruption but to heal confusion.

I looked up as pale headlights slid across the dark, glistening pavement. The taxi driver pulled up and stepped out, his eyes scanning the nearly empty parking lot. I forced a bright smile. He was working at three in the morning—that didn't sound like the best time either.

"Thanks so much for coming to get me," I said as he offered me his arm for support. I shakily stood up from the wheelchair. "You're working early!"

He nodded. "Are you here all alone?"

I nodded, still smiling. The smile wasn't fake—it was a small, trembling act of resistance—resistance against the catheter, the nurses' laughter, the bathroom scene—it was a way of saying, there is good, even in the bad here.

The taxi driver and I talked during the short drive home. He glanced over a few times. "You're a very cheerful person," he said. "Not many people smile on their way home from the hospital."

I laughed, trying to hold my body upright against the weariness that pulled at my shoulders. There are nights when your smile is shaky, your legs weaker than they should be, you feel at the limit of your strength, and your words aren't heard by those who should hear them. And yet, even then, in the darkness, at 2:00 a.m., your pain is seen. *You are seen by the God who never misses a single moment of faithfulness.* God does not waste fearful courage.

Scripture reminds us that "the LORD is near to the brokenhearted and saves the crushed in spirit" (Psalm 34:18 ESV). He does not diagnose you wrongly. He does not dismiss *your* pain. Jesus never looks at you and says, "Just get over it. Pull yourself up by your bootstraps . . . maybe join a support group? Because I don't know what else to do with you here." Instead, He enters your pain. He bears it. And *He* carries you through it.

When you feel misdiagnosed, misunderstood, mislabeled, when you walk or limp or crawl in brokenness through long and painful nights, or pass quietly by people who don't see you—*know* that you are seen. And your quiet acts—your shaky smiles, your deep breaths, your getting out of bed—will not be wasted by the God who never misses a single act of faithfulness. He glorifies with a spiritual glory your small moments of fierce, white-knuckled hope.

When we pulled up to my studio, the taxi driver parked and shook his head. "Don't worry about the fare," he said. "The smile was enough."

TEN

hope

Colton's voice came through the phone, flat and matter-of-fact. Surely I hadn't heard him right. "Our deployment is extended," he said. "Indefinitely."

My breath caught in my throat. He had *one month left*. One month.

"But . . . how can it be extended?"

"You know what's happening here," Colton said. "Sending troops home from a border country in the middle of a war would be a mistake. It looks like weakness. We have to stay. No one knows for how long."

I clutched the phone to my ear, staring at the wall in disbelief. I understood the unrest, the mounting tension near Colton's station, culminating at last in Russia's invasion of Ukraine. Poland bordered Ukraine, and thousands of refugees were pouring into Poland to seek aid from the US military. Colton's unit had been ordered to stay for assistance, for medical service, and—at the very least—a show of force.

"You've already been there for nine months," I said, desperation rising in my voice. "Why can't they send the next unit? Why does it have to be you guys?"

"Because if they sent a replacement, we'd still have to come back first," Colton said. "They would still be sending soldiers home. Still look weak. That wouldn't make sense."

I felt sick. Indefinitely? What does that even mean? No end in sight? No day count to hold on to?

"I can't do this indefinitely," I whispered, anger starting to fill my chest. "I've barely made it through this last month. I don't have anything left."

"You have to," Colton said. "We don't have a choice."

Every time things had felt impossible, I told myself, *Just two months left . . . just six weeks left . . . just one month left.* Now the thought haunted, sickening, exhausting: *No end in sight. This is life for . . . who knows how long?*

The stress made my symptoms worse. I typed out an email to my history professor, asking to be excused from the next day of class. "I don't ask for this lightly . . . circumstances outside my control . . . very difficult . . . physically and mentally . . . could I request a weeklong extension? . . . I wouldn't normally ask . . ."

I hit send. Then, the next day, I went to class anyway. What else could I do? Lying in bed, trying to process, made it worse. I couldn't afford to sit still and let the future swallow me. I had to keep moving. One day, one class, one step at a time.

This—I fumed, my mind filling with every crushing disappointment of the last five years—*this is why I don't trust happiness.*

Promises

"Please shade in the areas where you are in pain."

I stared at the figure outline on the medical form and shaded in the whole thing. Head, yes. Arms, legs. Hands and fingers, yes, yes. Torso, definitely. Feet. Where do I color in for skin? For muscle? For nerve endings? *These should come with anatomical layers,* I mused. I put the pen down and waited for the physical therapist to join me.

I had been on the waitlist for this appointment for months, during which time I used every spare moment researching my illness. The more I learned, the more it felt like falling down an endless rabbit hole—enlightening, exhilarating, and terrifying all at once.

Functional neurological disorder used to be called "conversion disorder." This I already knew because some doctors still used the term with me. The name came from Sigmund Freud's theory of psychological conversion—the idea that mental anguish could "convert" into unexplained physical symptoms.

Ever since learning this, I had harbored a deep and abiding disdain of Sigmund Freud. How had a long-dead, outdated psychological theorist obsessed with the unconscious and Oedipus complex managed to keep such a stranglehold on contemporary medicine? Healthy me couldn't have imagined having such a strong personal opinion on the late psychologist. Reading *The Interpretation of Dreams* in high school summarized the extent of my Freudian knowledge. But now, his theories burrowed into every corner of my life and illness—twisting my treatment from doctors, fueling the stigma that surrounded my symptoms, breeding disbelief.

His theory shaped every condescending dismissal, every accusation of malingering, every doctor who passed me on from psychoanalyst to neurologist and back again to psychoanalyst like an exasperating problem. Even my personal struggle of processing and accepting my own diagnosis—the hours I spent researching the information about my disease that no doctor seemed to know or care to tell me—stemmed from the ideas of this one man, dead for eighty years. *Sigmund Freud,* I mused, fidgeting on the blue vinyl seats of the clinic chairs. *I wish I could find a doctor with a very specific amnesia who's never heard of him.*

I hadn't known before that the roots of this mindset stretched even deeper, back long before Freud. All the way back to the Greeks, the problem had been known as *hysteria*, also—according to the Greeks—a feminine problem. The word *hysteria* itself comes from the Greek word *hyster* or uterus. Ancient physicians believed a woman's womb could roam throughout her body, causing all kinds of strange and unexplainable problems. For centuries, *hysteria* remained a convenient label for anything that defied easy medical explanation.

The consequences were real. In the nineteenth and early twentieth centuries, an alarming number of women were prescribed hysterectomies to "cure" what we now recognize as epilepsy, depression, schizophrenia, or—ironically—even infertility. And yet, the theory of hysteria remains. I feel the effect palpably, every time I go to the ER.

Hopefully this physical therapist will be different. I let out my breath in a silent prayer. *Please, let her know something true about FND.* Nonetheless, I steeled myself before she walked in. If she turned me out the door after looking at my medical forms, I couldn't say I hadn't seen it coming.

Parts of the medical field still label FND as psychological, not because anyone has *explained* it psychologically, but because no one has explained it *physically*. Recent fMRI studies of patients with FND, however, have revealed what traditional scans never could: the tangible, neurological changes of FND. You can *see* it—irregularities in white and gray brain matter ratios, an enlarged amygdala, disrupted coordination between automatic and conscious neural pathways. Brain regions responsible for emotion and those processing sensory input, movement, and pain overlap abnormally.

Theories are still being posited based on this research—physical causes, not mental. Everything from protein production, translation from DNA to RNA, an anatomical predisposition in the brain, and epigenetics. Yet old-school doctors seem to hold most fast to the one thing *disproven* in every recent study: *purely psychological causation.* The manifestation of the disease can be *physically* seen with the fMRI machine—inexplicably, a machine almost *never* used to secure a diagnosis.

The more I researched—poring over pages of medical studies, journals, private articles, newspapers—the clearer it became: FND does not have a purely psychological foundation but a neurological one. I have a brain-processing disorder. One that manifested in physical symptoms because something happened to me *physically.*

For decades, the medical field has been divided between the old perspective and the emerging one— up to about ten years ago. Studies track a correlation between FND and trauma, but not a connection strong enough to prove causation. Only half of FND patients have any former trauma to speak of, and often, little more can be shown to prove a connection beyond the timing of symptom onset. Ironically, most neurological diseases have trauma as a risk factor, including those for which we *know* the physical cause—such as multiple sclerosis, Parkinson's, or dementia. Trauma heightens the risk factor for most chronic illnesses. Trauma can flip the switch, but it isn't the electricity. It isn't the cause.

I closed my eyes. *Please, may this physical therapist be up-to-date on the research,* I prayed. *Please let her know what this actually is, so she can help me.*

The door opened to reveal a young, bright-eyed woman with a petite frame and a springy step. Her curly hair was tied back in a low ponytail. She smiled at me.

"You must be Sydney," she said. "I'm Rachel. Let's talk about your symptoms."

We went over the paperwork together, and she paused when she reached the body diagram I'd shaded in.

"I notice you've marked everything," she said, looking up at me. "That must be hard. Can you tell me more about what your pain is like?"

The more we talked, the more relieved I felt. *I think she's listening. I think she believes me.*

"I'm not a specialist in FND," she admitted, "but I have known and helped several patients with this neurological disorder."

She said "neurological." My heart pounded.

"Your brain is like a computer," she continued.

Yes, yes, I know where she's going with this.

"With functional neurological disorder, there's nothing wrong with the hardware of your brain. The software is what's malfunctioning. Something disrupted the way your brain processes movement and sensation, which engraved incorrect neural pathways. The longer it goes on, the more deeply those pathways get stuck."

I nodded. *She knows. She knows.*

"If it's okay with you, I'd like to check something called Hoover's sign," she said, getting up from her seat.

I nodded again. I knew about Hoover's sign—a diagnostic test for FND. No doctor had ever tried it on me before—including the one who diagnosed me—but I had researched it and noticed its effects in myself.

"Which leg is weaker right now?" she asked.

"My right."

"Okay. Try lifting it."

I lifted it to show her. My right leg began tremoring and spasming uncontrollably.

"Now tap your *other* foot on the floor to this rhythm." She tapped my left knee to a quiet, steady beat. I followed the pattern. Almost immediately, the tremors in my right leg slowed, then stopped. The moment I stopped tapping my left foot, the spasming began again.

She stepped back and nodded. "This is a neurological test of involuntary symptoms—tremors, paralysis, tics, things like that. In FND, these symptoms persist no matter how much you try to stop them, but when your brain is distracted—like when you were tapping just now—the movements often reduce or disappear. When your focus returns, so do the symptoms."

I hesitated. "I heard before that Hoover's sign proves FND is purely psychological. That the symptoms stop because they're all in my head. Why does distraction work?" I knew the answer. I needed to hear her say it. *Please tell me it's not psychological*, I breathed. *Please know the reason why too.*

She shook her head. "FND is not purely psychological. Your brain is misfiring signals to your nervous system because the way it processes movement and control has been disrupted. Your brain has two pathways for movement: automatic and focused. Automatic movements—walking, picking something up, even swinging your legs when you sit—happen without us thinking. They live in our parasympathetic nervous system, alongside things like breathing and your heartbeat." She smiled. "Ever been walking and felt someone watching you? And then, all at once, you forgot how to walk?"

I laughed. "Yes!"

"That's your brain switching from automatic to focused. We're not as practiced in focused pathways, so suddenly, walking feels unnatural. With FND, it's like your brain is stuck in one state. It tries so hard to consciously control movements that they become tangled and distorted. That's why distraction works—it briefly pulls your brain out of that overfocus, allowing normal movement to resume temporarily. But as soon as your attention returns to the movement, the misfiring starts again."

I exhaled slowly. "So my brain physically can't move itself back to automatic processing?"

"Correct," she said. "Everything—walking, speaking, sensory processing, even pain responses—gets stuck in that overworked, focused state. Your brain is trying so hard to get the right signals through that many of them become jumbled or misdirected. That's why FND symptoms often don't have a clear physical cause. Your brain looks structurally healthy, but it's lost the proper neural pathways. We have to retrain it."

"Okay." I breathed out slowly, a weight lifting from my shoulders. "How do we do that?"

For the first time in the presence of a medical professional, I let myself think: *This is not my fault. It's real. Something is wrong with how my brain is working. It's not just in my head.*

She leaned forward. "We use your brain's distraction bias to our advantage. Every part of retraining will incorporate distraction. Let's aim for ten weeks."

"Ten weeks? Really?" I could not keep the hopefulness and surprise out of my voice. *Could I be better in ten weeks?* The thought felt too good to be true. *Don't trust it,* I warned myself. *Don't trust the happiness. It will hurt too much if it fails.*

But when I got home that afternoon and sat at my desk, trying to study Thucydides, a deep ache spread through my chest and stomach. *I could get better.* The thought overwhelmed me. My hope had already fastened to it. I began to cry, pleading with God: *Please let this be true. Please let this be true.*

There's a breed of hope that feels almost unbearable. It surges up against your will, after you've taught yourself not to get attached. It pulses like a bruise when touched. You wade through hot, dry sand in the desert of your longing, feeling your mouth salivate while telling yourself the water you see is just a mirage. Hope feels dangerous to believe in. Hope feels like a fool's errand, guided by naivete, innocence—the baby, unbroken, unshattered version of yourself. If you shatter again, you're not sure you will survive.

I felt it then on that rolling desk chair, Thucydides' writings open and unread in front of me: If this longing was dashed to pieces, I would be dashed with it.

Practice

I stood on my left foot, right foot hovering in the air, knees wobbling as I clung to the wall. Exhaling slowly, I forced my eyes shut. All sense of where my legs were vanished. The ground beneath me seemed to disappear. I swayed, then felt myself falling. My eyes flew open as I caught myself against the wall, both feet slamming back onto the carpet, legs trembling.

"Your brain's proprioception is damaged," Rachel had explained. "It's lost awareness of where your limbs are in space. You don't even realize how much you've started relying on visual cues to stay upright. That's why closing your eyes—or moving in the dark—feels impossible."

One of my first exercises was balancing on one foot and practicing movements with my eyes closed. Stripping away the visual crutch on which my brain had grown dependent was harder than I expected. I planted both feet, shut my eyes again, and hovered my hands off the wall. Even standing still with both feet on the ground felt like balancing on tiny pegs over the surface of the carpet. My ankles wobbled like the neck of a bobblehead doll. The moment I lost spatial awareness, a wave of panic surged through me—like teetering on the edge of a cliff. Again and again, I caught myself at the last second, gripping the wall before I fell.

Will it always feel like this? Like I'm falling? I had heard of patients with FND experiencing functional blindness—where their brain, without warning, shut off their ability to see. No physical cause. No clear way to fix it.

A shudder ran through me. What if that happens to me? What if I lose every bit of orientation I have left?

Under the Microscope

Despite the difficulty of the exercises, I felt stronger the next few days. The hope of getting better was euphoric. I worked hard. I even walked places without my cane. I didn't hallucinate or lose presence of mind. I didn't spiral. My pain decreased.

On the one hand, I was elated. I felt powerful, invincible, grateful, remade. I wanted to shout to the world that I was getting better. I wanted to run for miles without my cane, to walk the streets and leave Jeeves behind at home, to push the limits of my strength. I wanted to stay up all night cramming for school, drinking in the energy I had missed for so long.

On the other hand, there was a strange wariness—a tinge of wonder, anticipation, even a sense of loss.

I felt my identity wobbling on the edge. Am I sick, or am I better? Am I still disabled, or am I healed? Should I still carry my cane, leave the room for seizures, and rest because I need to? Or am I allowed again to push the limits of my strength and revel in it, as I did when I was well? Should I bring my cane to school, or would I be a fraud to carry it out of cautious habit? Did I start physical therapy only to prove I never needed it?

I questioned so much. Were the months of falling, paralysis, and losing myself again and again just a prelude to a sudden, miraculous cure? Or was I not doing as well as I thought I was, and the crash was just around the corner? Perhaps I had grown so used to being sick that any lesser version of pain felt like recovery.

There's a quiet, disorienting grief that can come with getting better. Especially when your suffering has carved out who you are—how you speak, where you go, what you expect from yourself and your body, how other people see you. Healing, even when you've longed for it, can feel like stepping out of a story you've spent months or years writing. And in that in-between space, before the dust has settled at your feet, you can start to wonder: *Who am I now? Who will I be if this healing lasts?*

Like living with an abusive parent, suffering feels like home. The violence of life becomes something you brace yourself for—even expect. It conditions you to believe its honesty, even if you hate its torture. I've felt drawn toward depression even as I've loathed it. So much of me had been swallowed by it, I wondered if there would be anything left if it disappeared. I wanted to get better—to escape the darkness, the power of the disease—but I didn't remember who I was before it. Who was I before I was sad, riven, wanting to die? Perhaps I was nothing. Perhaps I was boring. Perhaps I was a failure all along and didn't know it.

Anxiety may be the hated voice in your head, but have you ever wondered if, without it, your mind would go silent? You might hate the pain, the disability, the cane, the wheelchair—but who are you without the familiarity of your own particular suffering? You've experienced the death you never asked for, but rebirth can be just as painful, just as disorienting. You are being made new. Maybe. The newness is as frightening as the maybe.

It had taken months to accept that I was disabled and that I may never get better. Now it seemed just as earth-shifting, identity-shattering, to recognize that I might, in fact, get well—that I might have already started. Perhaps in a few months I would never need a cane, never be in pain, never have seizures. I realize now, looking back, how much of my identity was still rooted in my own strength. I had lost *physical* capacity—the ability to walk, and hike, and train, and venture out like I used to. Even the ability, sometimes, to so much as make a peanut butter sandwich in the kitchen. But because I was set back so far into physical weakness, anything I accomplished—staying in college, living alone, passing exams, making it through Colton's deployment—was itself an exaltation of my inner strength and courage to those around me. I was an exceptional student with a disability, an average student without one. I was an inspiration just for living with a disability, but living is not enough if you are well. I was a strong wife now—facing my first year of illness alone while my husband was deployed overseas, but our whole marriage had been made fast in the cords of shared struggle. What would our marriage be like if we didn't *need* each other, if we were not lashed together like two creaking beams in a hurricane? Could love, only built in the storm, last without one? Whenever your identity, your security, your strength is found in something that is not Christ, change—good or bad—will always upend you. You can spend years making peace with who you are only to find that "getting better" asks you to become someone else all over again. You are forced to release what became familiar, even sacred, in your pain. You are forced to ask: *Who am I without this?*

Happiness can feel unfamiliar—like something dangerous instead of safe. Because you know pain. You've made a home inside it. And when that starts to shift, you don't feel pure relief as you imagined; instead you feel disoriented. Recovery should feel like regaining, but sometimes it feels like erasure. And I don't think it's because you love the pain. I think it's because the pain feels so intense, so real, so terrible, that you start to believe it matters more than you do.

Pain

I remember the exact moment it started: when I was exercising. I lifted my right leg, and a thin thread of numbness traveled above my left calf, over my thigh, up to my hip. It was just one thread, strange and tingling, but I noticed it. Within a few seconds, my leg felt dead—numb from thigh to ankle, a strange space disconnected to my body, except for the faintest sensation of floor beneath the sole of my foot.

I finished the workout as best I could, but my walking didn't recover.

I didn't let myself think the relapse would have any lasting effect on my overall recovery. In some ways, it came almost as a relief. For the past few days, I had felt like I was under a microscope. Someone from my school had stopped me the night before and said he'd heard I went to class without my cane. He'd "heard it from Gabe." But Gabe wasn't in my class, so who had Gabe heard it from? I was walking with my cane again when we spoke, but my steps were smooth, steady. I felt suspended in a strange in-between space. If I agreed that I was doing better, then I wasn't protecting my right to relapse later if it happened. If I disagreed, I risked sounding ungrateful—or like an impostor.

It had taken courage to go to school without my cane. I almost regretted it the moment I stepped outside. I had to go back home after class to get it for the rest of the day. Maybe I shouldn't have done it, but I wanted to see if I could walk without it. I wished I could take the small risks without being labeled as either "sick" or "recovered."

The ups and downs of recovery can be so violent, so unexpected, so identity-shifting, so analyzed, parsed, judged, and inspected by everyone around you. They can make you want to close off, to always use a cane—literal or figurative—until you never need one again. It can feel easier to just show up one day and say, "Yes, I am well now," and know it is true, with no disclaimer or reservations, and have them ask how you did it once it was done, not while you are still fighting.

Relapse can feel like betrayal—but it can also feel like familiar ground. It can feel like failure while also feeling routine. Relapse is both horribly redundant and intimately recognizable. It is the *usual* in all the profound, timeworn seasoning of that word.

Courage doesn't always look like walking without a cane. Sometimes it looks like using it again.

Your life might be full of moments like this one—full of light and music and snow and coffee, full of loneliness, holding both beauty and heartbreak. You may feel as though you're suspended in contradiction: your body breaking down, your mind grasping for peace, your spirit straining toward something unspoken—maybe something you've never seen or had or felt.

So often we think the beauty has to come *after* the redemption. After the symptoms cease. After the healing is final and undeniable.

But that is not how God works. The beauty begins now. Not because the relapse is beautiful—not because the pain is good—but because your Redeemer is already at work, even here.

Redemption begins before the restoration is visible. That future glory for which we wait is not frozen in the distance—it reaches backward into our suffering and transforms it even now. *In the relapse.* We see our setbacks as the cancellation of our progress. Our limps—physical or spiritual—as disqualifying our bravery. Our relapses as erasing our growth. We think we must explain, justify—pick a lane: "sick" or "well"—but we don't have to. We are allowed to live in tension. In fact, that is the only place we're able to live. Until heaven.

God brings glory to the in-between. To the blank page between the Old and New Testaments, when His children waited four hundred years in darkness and silence. He brings glory to the Holy Saturday when Jesus was dead in the tomb, and the whole world heaved a long, aching breath, suspended between death and resurrection. God brings glory to the moments of suspension, of apparent contradiction, the pendulous swing of pain and promise that never, in this life, settles quite in the middle.

The next day was Saturday. I wondered if I would be able to walk.

If not, I had done this before. And I was not afraid.

ELEVEN

wheelchair

I needed a wheelchair long before I got one. In the end, it was Dr. Schlect's history field trip that pushed me—quite literally—over the edge. The yearlong history colloquium is a cornerstone of New Saint Andrews College, and the history field trip is its grand finale. Our class had been talking about it for months—a sixteen-hour, jam-packed expedition through battlefields and ancient Nez Perce village sites, tracing the legends woven into the Palouse hills, all while looping through Northern Idaho, from Moscow to White Bird Canyon, to Kamiah, back again in one big bus. It was the kind of immersive, rigorous experience that makes history real to both student and teacher—real, recent, and riveting.

From the beginning, I assumed I wouldn't be able to go. The schedule alone—starting at four in the morning—was enough to knock me out of the running. Mornings were often when my symptoms hit hardest, and even on a good day, I couldn't manage that much walking—much less go for that long without a seizure episode. I told myself I wouldn't want to make anyone else uncomfortable, but truly,

I just hated feeling vulnerable—and there is nothing more vulnerable than lying belly up, a shaking, shivering, helpless mass in front of a whole bus of people you know.

I emailed Dr. Schlect regarding the field trip, asking the question I knew the answer to already: "Will the day have a lot of walking?" I expected a quick *yes*—an easy way out—and had my polite decline drafted in my head. I braced myself to miss yet another big moment with my classmates and was already preparing to ask for a revised final exam, being that ours relied on the field trip for its analysis. *At least this one is cut-and-dried*, I thought after I clicked send on the email. *There's just no possible way I could swing this.*

Dr. Schlect, however, wasn't so sure. "Yes, there is a lot of walking involved," he emailed back. "Intermingled with a lot of sitting on the bus. And it is a very long day. You and I should discuss this. There may be some creative ways we could make accommodations?"

Creative ways? I wondered. Flying carpet aside, I couldn't imagine any way creative enough to remove walking from a sixteen-hour field trip. And even if we could somehow eliminate walking, what about seizures? What about areas that were not accessible? What about the sheer exertion the day demanded? I agreed to meet with Dr. Schlect, quietly planning to behead any creativity with a very practical axe.

The first book we had read under Dr. Schlect's guidance was the writing of Herodotus, the *Pater Historiae*, he had told us—the Father of History. Through the course, Dr. Schlect himself became our *Pater Historiae*—witty, engaging, and inexhaustible. Behind every word he spoke lay a quiet mountain of history, a lifetime of reading and thinking. Prick him, and he bled stories. He never simply *taught* history; he unfolded it, made it tangible, weaving narratives so compelling that our toes curled under our desk seats and our hearts pounded. After a two-hour class with Dr. Schlect, we walked out of the classroom buzzing in an absorbing, adrenaline-fueled fog, the salt-spray from ancient Greek triremes still bitter on our lips. So, really, I should have known.

I should have known that when I sat down in Dr. Schlect's office to explain why this trip would be impossible, I was talking to a man whose mind was full of stories of things that had seemed impossible once—but happened anyway.

The Plunge

Team Sydney.

The subject line of the email stared back at me. It was addressed to me and six young men from my class—volunteers willing to get me and a wheelchair up a mountain.

Dr. Schlect laid out the plan: "The goal is to minimize Sydney's exertion through the day. This means using her wheelchair at every possible opportunity . . . Many hands make light work—divide the duties, take turns . . ."

The meeting with Dr. Schlect had not gone as I expected. He greeted me with a smile and a twinkle in his eye, excitement at the challenge before us infused into every word.

"I'm thinking this," he began, spreading out his hands wide in front of him. "We get you a wheelchair that's stowed in the bottom of the bus. At every stop, a group of volunteers will unload the wheelchair, set it up, and take turns pushing you. If there are enough volunteers, this would mean finagling you through places otherwise inaccessible. We will prep the group on your seizures in case you have one, but any stop that feels like too much you can sit through on the bus. You can also leave the group at any point if you feel a seizure coming on, and sit at the front of the bus so we can help provide privacy should one happen on the drive. Most importantly, we will have a group of people whose primary focus is *you*—getting Sydney over all the bumps and hurdles of the field trip with as little exertion as possible. Does this sound like it would work?"

I hesitated. He had prepared a solution to nearly every obstacle, but there was still one, overarching problem I could not see any way around.

"Yes . . . but I just—I struggle with being a burden. I don't like accepting help."

"Yes, well," Dr. Schlect said, leaning back in his chair with a smile. "You will need to get over that."

I looked at the email now, unfolding the day's strategy: "A key to pulling this off is for you all to have fun with it. Moving Sydney should become 'the game within the game,' a special project that elevates the whole group. If you go about it the right way, this can become a highlight reel for the trip that everyone will remember."

My only job was to find a wheelchair. Even with the severity of my daily symptoms, my first instinct was to rent one. I called around town, trying to find what it would take to rent a wheelchair for a day. The options were all wrong—big, clunky manual chairs, none of which were suited for trails or thick grass. They were also expensive—hundreds of dollars for a single day. No delivery. How was I even supposed to pick one up without a car, by myself? And then return it afterward?

Unless . . . The thought hit me. Maybe I shouldn't be trying to rent a wheelchair. Maybe I should be *buying* one.

No. No, that's not necessary yet. I slammed my laptop shut and looked around my studio apartment—the rolling desk chair I maneuvered across the floor, the hardwood I'd collapsed on too many times, the space between me and the bathroom, the kitchen in the corner that felt impervious on so many long days and nights. *But I can still walk,* I reasoned. *Maybe not all the time—but enough. And I am managing . . . sort of.* Besides, wasn't a rolling desk chair basically the same thing? Was there really that much of a difference?

Yes. Yes, there was. A rolling desk chair could never take me outside. It could never get me through this field trip. It couldn't even get me over the carpet—I always had to stop four feet away from my mattress, throw myself off, and shimmy the rest of the way on my stomach. Colton called me "the salmon," a nickname that felt both insulting and accurate. Many nights, I flopped my way from the floor up onto the mattress, like a fish struggling upstream.

Maybe I could just look at prices. It might be cheaper than renting. I opened the laptop again and hesitated. Where does someone even buy a wheelchair? Amazon?

Turns out, Amazon has them. Manual wheelchairs. Big and bulky, many of them—but cheaper than renting and closer to the size I needed. I let out my breath. *I can order a wheelchair, have it sent right to my door, and send it back for a refund if it doesn't work for me.*

Buying a wheelchair was actually the option with the least risk. I pulled up the cheapest one available—a standard Medline, black, with a vinyl back and seat, extended leg rests, forty-five pounds: $160.

Click. Done. Bought.

Just for the field trip, I reassured myself.

Wheelchair

Everyone tells you to ease into your first use of a mobility aid. Start somewhere familiar. Keep outings short. Don't draw attention. Get used to it alone. No one recommends making your first public use of a wheelchair being carried—literally—up a mountain, by a team of eight or nine men, in front of twenty students, over the course of sixteen hours.

Exposure therapy at its finest.

I tried the wheelchair in my studio first, filming the moment, determined to create something encouraging for other mobility-aid users. But as soon as I saw myself in the chair, I broke down in tears. I couldn't stop staring. The eighteen-inch seat swallowed me whole, the armrests were bulky, and the leg rests stuck out, extending almost two feet in front. I spent two days trying to convince myself it was perfect before sending it back and ordering a sixteen-inch model. It felt much better. I was grateful I'd bought it from Amazon, where returns and exchanges were fast and easy. The process was unconventional, maybe, but for someone who couldn't drive, it worked.

I spent time staring at myself in the mirror from the vinyl seat. I adjusted what I could. The armrests were the first to go—too bulky, and I never used them anyway. That alone made a huge difference in the "swallowing" effect. I wished I could tuck the leg rests under the seat instead of having them extend out in front. They also added almost ten pounds, making the chair heavier and harder to maneuver, but removing them meant keeping my legs dangling above the floor, a position both painful and fatiguing. I placed a black faux-leather dining chair cushion on the seat and hooked a small, rose-gold backpack over the handles.

Cute . . . I think. I'd make it work.

That first night, I rolled around my studio to get used to how it felt beneath me—trying to have fun with it. I sped over the smooth wood floors, skidding to a stop. I attempted donuts and wheelies—landing flat on my back on the first try. I spun in circles and wove in and out serpentine style. The feeling of moving across these floors—over which I had struggled for so many hours—was euphoric. There was no struggle. Just freedom. Speed. I held my breath and wheeled over the threshold into the bathroom. Then over the carpet to my bed. Effortless.

Okay. Maybe this *was* better than the rolling desk chair.

I will use it for the field trip and only when I absolutely can't walk, I promised myself. *After this trip, I will never use it in public. I won't go anywhere I can't maneuver on my own. I will use my cane as much as possible. I will keep going to physical therapy until I can leave all mobility aids behind.*

"That's fine, babe, that's fine," Colton said when I told him the rules I had made for myself. "I'm just glad you got it—at least for your really bad days. I'll feel better knowing you're not going to fall anymore."

Field Trip

The day of the field trip dawned sharp and cold—Moscow in mid-April. It started easily enough. Our first stop was a museum and historical society outside Lewiston. Most of the paths were smooth, and my classmates took turns pushing me along without trouble.

"We're cruisin'!" Micah laughed from behind me. "You know what would be cool? If they made motorized wheelchairs. You know, like wheelchairs that push themselves. Or even all-terrain wheelchairs!"

I laughed too. "They actually make all of those," I said. "They just cost a lot more than $160 on Amazon."

"That's so cool! Have you ever thought about entering the Paralympics?"

I grinned again. People always seem to ask this of disabled people but never think of wondering aloud to the average healthy person if they'll enter the Olympics.

"Maybe," I joked. The ride was easy—until we reached the grass. By then, my designated driver had switched.

"Thanks, Sam." I laughed nervously as he pushed me over the jarring turf of a Nez Perce village site. "This is not something I take *lightly*." I heard the jerky breath behind me catch in a pity-chuckle. We arrived behind everyone at the Indian Agency cabin, and I stared momentarily through the rough-cut doorway that had stood for the last one hundred sixty years.

"Built in 1862," Dr. Schlect explained, as Sam heaved my wheelchair over the split log that formed the threshold to the newly constructed concrete floor inside. He grinned. "Sorry they didn't build this with wheelchairs in mind." I prided myself on the way back to the bus that I had leaned into the awkwardness of the challenging moments with humor and gratitude rather than embarrassment and apologies.

Surely the hardest parts of the trip are over, I thought. *Nothing can be much more inaccessible than the uneven grounds they've pushed me over so far.* For about ten hours, I was correct. We stood near Hatwai Creek as Dr. Schlect retold the ancient Nez Perce legends from which the surrounding hills had gotten their names: Coyote, Short-Faced Bear, Mammoth.

Miss Frog, the boulder at the bottom, crouched in a most unseemly manner—which made sense as her story was full of immodesties. Evan clutched my wheelchair back as we scrambled down the steep boat ramp to the mammoth graveyard lying beneath the glassy surface of the frigid Tolo Lake. We stood on the cliff overlooking the grave of the unknown soldier, desecrated after settlers realized the soldier was not a white man but a Native American who had acquired a soldier's coat and sidearm.

But then we entered White Bird Battlefield: the mountain we'd need to climb. A rough, grass-covered trail wound up the steep hillside, and I could hear the labored breathing of the guys behind me. One of them pushed the wheelchair forward, tilting the front wheels off the ground at times to navigate the denser patches of grass or rutted turf. Through the thicker sections, another guy joined him, one handle each. I clung to the sides of the chair, swaying and jolting through each labored stride. I would have felt ashamed at the heavy breathing behind me if we had not taken Dr. Schlect's words to heart. It was a game. The guys wheezed out jokes and cheerful whistles between the evasive gasps, and before long, one of them struck up a song. The rest of us joined in; six exultant voices laughed and sang up the rough mountainside. Classmates far ahead of us turned back with smiles to watch and join in. Every time we made it over a tough patch, I lifted my arm in victory and we all cheered.

About two-thirds of the way through, what was left of our winding, grassy trail ended in a terrain of rocky ledges and stony ground—steeper than anything we'd pushed through yet. The guy behind me stopped and I put on the brake of my wheelchair to keep from rolling backward. The six of us stared at the seemingly impossible mile that remained. Somewhere up there, Dr. Schlect was still leading us forward, weaving our own story into all those that belonged to the mountainside.

We stood for a moment, shooting off ideas. Could I walk if two guys supported me, one on each side? Would a piggyback ride be wildly inappropriate? Of all the ideas bandied back and forth, staying there or turning back wasn't considered. We had made it this far, and if we had learned anything from Dr. Schlect, it was that no adventure has ever existed without a few boulders in the way.

I started shivering, my muscles going spastic with the tremors. Evan looked at me, took off his jacket, and put it over my shoulders. "We'll carry her," he said, laughing. The others grinned, took off their jackets, and piled them all on top of me. Four pairs of hands grabbed the frame of my chair and lifted me off the ground. The air rang with cheers. I was weightless in space, a princess in a litter, sailing a ship through the air. I was riding a flying carpet over White Bird Battlefield.

Step by step, they carried me up the mountain. When we reached the summit, the entire class erupted in cheers. The guys set me down, faces flushed, breathless but triumphant. Their pride was contagious. What started as my challenge had become everyone's. It belonged to all of us.

Halfway through the descent, I felt a seizure coming on.

I turned to Joe, the guy closest to me. "I think I'm about to have a seizure."

He nodded. "All right, let's find a good place to set her down," he called out. "She's going to have a seizure." I had warned them this might happen. They knew what to do. They carried me off the trail, lowering the chair before helping me to the ground. I pulled myself to the side so I could lean against a wheel, trying to steady my breath.

"I'm okay," I managed, forcing a smile. They backed up, giving me space. Some turned away to offer privacy, while others watched from a distance, curious but quiet. The seizure trembled through—mild, nothing violent or long.

"Interesting," Evan said as they helped me into the wheelchair. I leaned back, weak and exhausted. Jubal took off running down the hill and came back a few minutes later.

"I got this from the bus," he said, pressing a cold water bottle into my hands. He had run half a mile for it—and I hadn't even asked. I drank gratefully. Then, with a deep breath, I nodded.

"All right, let's go!" Joe shouted. They lifted the wheelchair again, carrying me the rest of the way down. By the time the bus arrived back in town, it was almost midnight. We were exhausted. Exhilarated. At the final exam, when students were asked about the highlight of the term, many of them answered the same way: "Getting Sydney up the mountain."

"When you push away help because you're afraid of being a burden," Dr. Schlect had told me, "you rob others of the blessing of helping you."

I carry those words with me, even now.

Blessings Through Burdens

Asking for help feels dangerous. It's an admission of need. A surrender of control. Fighting past the quiet, aching fear that if you let yourself lean on others, they might resent the weight. That the absolute worst feeling in the world would be handing someone your heart and having them roll their eyes and hand it back to you. You don't want your pain to inconvenience someone. You don't want your neediness to outlast their compassion.

That day, I could have stayed behind instead of scaling the mountain. I could have said, *No, Dr. Schlect. Thank you, but it's too much. I don't want to be a burden. You all go on ahead.* I wanted to say that; it's what I had planned. But if he had listened, we would have lost the story.

Because the truth is, we were made to carry one another.

When you ask for help, you're not just admitting your need—you're inviting someone into a story bigger than any single person. You're giving someone the chance to step into kindness, into generosity, into love. You're letting someone experience the deep satisfaction of lifting another person—sometimes literally.

It doesn't always look dramatic. Clara once drove me around the neighborhood to look at fall leaves when I had been stuck inside for a week. Heidi named my cane. My friend Eden dropped off Easter dinner when I was in too much pain to make their invite. It's not easy. Vulnerability never is. But if you never ask for help, you never get to see the way people will rise to meet your weakness. You never get to witness the quiet endurance of friendship, of community, of strangers becoming teammates, of burdens becoming shared.

"I don't want to be a burden," I had told Lisa Leidenfrost over a cup of tea on that snowy afternoon.

I expected the usual reassurance: You are not a burden . . . Never be afraid of that.

Instead she said, "It's okay though. People are meant to be burdens."

Her words startled me. But she was right. It's part of the design—dependency. Even in Eden, before weakness, before sickness, before sin, God looked at a whole and healthy and perfect Adam and said, "It is not good that man should be alone" (Genesis 2:18).

So, He made a helper. God never wired us for independence. If you make independence the goal of your life and your pain, the proof of your victory, the banner of your success—you will never reach it, and you will be miserable the whole time you try.

Paul told us in Galatians 6:2, "Bear one another's burdens, and so fulfill the law of Christ." Burdens invite you to share in the picture of Christ. They are part of considering others above yourself. They are a natural extension of your need for God. Your dependency is not a flaw but a reflection of a cosmic-level truth: Neediness is God's idea.

TWELVE

reunion

I don't want to stay here," I told Colton emphatically on the phone. "School ends in two weeks, and after that, there's nothing keeping me here."

"Um . . . okay," Colton replied cautiously from the other end. Even our short marriage had taught him to expect any manner of wild ideas from me. He was good at hearing me out before telling me I was crazy.

"I've lived very carefully here," I said, determined to show how logical and thought through my plan was. "You know my expenses have been almost nothing."

He knew. Some of the other men at the barracks even suggested I had some "alternate source" of income while he was gone. The truth is, barely eating and having no car cuts down on living expenses a lot.

"We have some money saved because of that, and"—I rushed on, determined to get the words out—"I want to go somewhere. *Anywhere.* I want to carry on with my plans and goals and not let the Army stop them!"

There it was. The Army. After a long string of what felt like numerous broken promises and still no end in sight, I detested the control the Army held over our lives. It had forced this deployment, it had forced this whole last year of living alone, it had forced the misery, the floor fallings, the loneliness, our first anniversary, first Valentine's Day, first birthdays, the first year of marriage neither of us could have imagined, and now it deprived me of a countdown to the end. It did, however, offer "separation pay" for the trouble. Two hundred and fifty dollars. It felt like a slap in the face.

When you want to feel control again, you choose strange enemies. I couldn't fight my body, my pain, my suffering. But I could pin it all on one thing and fight that—the military. Many of us do that to something—we tend to make it significant by putting a capital letter up front. The Ex, that Church, the Accident, the Diagnosis, Cancer, the Job Loss, Insurance. It's easy to pin your frustration on something else, something tangible. It's easy to fight, and claw, and cast your hatred on a single event, person, or agency. It's easier to do that than to surrender to the God who holds *all things*—every piece of your suffering—in His hands.

"Where are you wanting to go?" Colton asked, his voice still cautious.

"Anywhere," I repeated. "I'd like to visit England again, like I did after high school. I loved Oxford. Or maybe someplace new, by the ocean."

"Why not here?"

"There?" I didn't know that was an option. During this whole period of separation, Poland had felt like Timbuktu. The Army had closed off the path to my husband for months. What could change?

"I don't know," Colton admitted when I asked him. "You couldn't stay on post, and I'm not allowed to leave post often. And when I do, it's only with other soldiers. But now that things are slowing down a bit, field trainings are over and such, I can sometimes get to Gorzów by train, the next town over. For a few hours at a time, at least. Maybe if you stayed there, sometimes we could see each other. Not for long, and no promises. But maybe."

The maybe was enough. Putin had nothing on me. I felt as if I was fighting the whole US Army all on my own.

My Cup of Noodle Water

The night before I was preparing to leave, I heard dripping. Dripping in my kitchen. With no man to call on, I dragged myself out of bed, hobbled over, and flipped on the light. A pool of water sat in the middle of the yellow vinyl kitchen floor, beneath a darkening, bubbling, sagging bulge on the ceiling. I grabbed a glass from the cabinet and set it under the drips, then headed out the door with Jeeves clumping at my side.

Since I was in room 103, I assumed the culprit was in 203. I climbed the stairs, went down the unfamiliar hallway, and stopped at the right door, expecting to knock as politely as I could at three in the morning and inform them that their faucet was running onto my kitchen floor.

I raised my hand to knock, then paused. The door was already open. I peeked through the crack. The room was trashed—piles of soggy clothes that smelled as if they were rotting, food on the carpet, empty and partially filled cups of various liquids scattered across nearby furniture. It was empty of people, as far as I could see, but that didn't seem like much to go on. Something was clearly wrong. And it was dripping into my kitchen.

Stepping back, I took a deep breath and called the non-emergency number of the police department. A few minutes later, I stood next to an older, mustached EMT outside the open door of the apartment. When the first EMT had gone in to scout out the room, we hadn't followed. I was afraid of finding a body. I glanced at the uniformed man next to me—perhaps he was too. "I found the source of the water!" We heard the shout from inside and glanced at each other.

"Where?" he asked after a moment's pause.

"Kitchen sink! It's running! It's plugged with—with, uh . . ."

"With *what*, Marcus?"

The tension in the room rose to an apex—the trash, the smell, the complete absence of any human explanation amid that chaos. The stagnant air started filtering out the door. Rotted food, damp clothes, dirty water. The faucet shut off in the kitchen.

"Marcus, with *what*?"

"Noodles, sir."

"Noodles?"

"Yes, sir. Spaghetti-type."

One of the EMTs came to check on my apartment before they left. The noodle water, still overflowing a bit upstairs, had now bubbled across the entire sagging ceiling and was pouring in sporadic bursts from the soggiest places above. Half a dozen perfect streams of water filled a pool across my vinyl floor, with my tiny glass cup standing in the middle of them, almost completely empty. Water was falling everywhere but into the cup.

The EMT and I both stood and looked at it for a moment, the one dry island in all that flood.

"That, um . . ." I began. "That was doing something when I put it there."

Often, we are that pathetic little cup, trying to catch the tidal wave of dirty water gushing from places we'd rather ignore.

I'll catch it. I'll hold it all. No one but me will get wet.

The problem is, nothing can hold all the bad you're up against. But it's not made to be held, contained. It's meant to be swallowed. That's the only way through the bad; someone must drink it.

"Father . . . take this cup away from Me," Jesus prayed in the garden. "Nevertheless not My will, but Yours, be done" (Luke 22:42).

Jesus swallowed evil whole by letting it swallow Him. He swallowed disability, divorce, death, and derangement. He swallowed ego, exhaustion, and empty promises. He swallowed failure, fear, and falling on cold apartment floors. He swallowed grief, greed, and deep, guttural groanings that cannot be uttered (Romans 8:26). He swallowed it whole, then rose from the dead, rose from that water—we call it baptism. Take your little cup and toss it out. Jesus calls you to simply trust that He has conquered the seas.

I grabbed two towels from the bathroom, hobbled over, and threw them onto the pool of water. They sank beneath the surface, submerged.

"I think I should move out tomorrow. Go overseas. Get out of the country."

The ceiling quietly bubbled in response.

Bag and Baggage

As soon as I announced my intentions to my family, my phone had been abuzz with calls and texts from people who loved me, telling me they wanted me safe, that my feelings were understandable and important, and that I was absolutely crazy. I nodded politely, said, "I know," and continued packing. *Crazy* was nothing new to me; it was the politest term one could use to describe the daily falls, getting stuck and paralyzed for hours on my own floor, belly-crawling to food and water, and resembling a floundering salmon trying to get onto my bed. At least this crazy might end in a hug.

It took three days for me to get overseas to Poland. The worst part of the trip, by far, was New York City. After landing at midnight and waiting for two hours to find an accessible taxi, a cab driver pushed me and my wheelchair into the trunk of his van and said, "I'd recommend brakes."

I sat on my wheelchair, no seat belt, no handles, and clung to the walls of the van to keep myself from tipping over. My suitcase slid across the cab floor and knocked against my footrest.

"Excuse me . . . sir?" I gasped. The van jostled us both to the right, and I nearly slammed into the window. "Is this . . . legal?"

He snorted as if offended. "I'm the only accessible cab you'll find this time of night," he said. Then added, in the tone of a man reading a script in a bad high school play: "I will always help the disabled."

I wanted to ask him if he had ever helped a passenger *become* disabled, but I decided the best course of action was to grit my teeth and try to survive the high-water voyage to the hotel. When we got there, he pulled my wheelchair, luggage, and me out of the trunk and set us all on the pavement. The ground tilted as if I had traveled by boat instead of taxi.

"I'll be back for the cash," he said. "Stay here."

"Accessibility" has dark corners.

"If you need the wheelchair lift, call for assistance," I've read on a sign outside the emergency room, facing two flights of stairs. Then I've waited ten minutes for someone to come get me, only to explain the lift to the ER was too sketchy (her words) to use anyway.

Our restaurant is fully accessible—except for the bathroom.

We meet ADA standards; three strange men who work here will carry you up the stairs.

Yes, we have one elevator, but it's been closed for maintenance for five months.

We do have an accessible entrance—around the back and through the trash bins.

There is an accessible route on campus. It involves wheeling your chair three miles around from the other side. What do you mean you can't do that? It's on a ramp!

In case of emergency, use stairs.

This is, without doubt, the best time in history to be disabled *by far*. I am so grateful. But we have a long way to go. Having real seats in taxis would be a good start.

I looked around the dark hotel parking lot. A black cat scurried out from underneath a broken-down Honda, glared at me with green eyes, then sprang back as the sounds of sudden shouting, falling metal, and swear words burst from the open carport across the street.

"Good. All this trip was lacking was a black cat."

When the taxi driver came back and I told him I needed to run inside for change, he accused me of stealing.

"You won't get away with this!" he shouted as I hurried inside to the ATM.

I pulled out sixty dollars and wheeled back to him.

"Disabled or not, you won't take advantage of me! You try to pull something like this, you'll never ride with me again."

Thank God, I thought, handing him the cash.

No Charming Men

I was seated on the plane next to a young business owner who claimed to be in marketing—stylish clothes, tailored and pressed, clean-cut beard, with a sleek watch glinting under his cuff. He flirted the entire six-hour flight, despite me telling him I was very happily married, and, in fact, on my way to Poland to see my husband who had been deployed for eleven months.

At this news, he leaned back in his seat and gave a low whistle. "Poland? Now *that's* love," he said. "I'd give anything for someone who'd fly across the world just to see me."

Well, sir, have you tried not flirting with married women?

He sipped on his whiskey—neat, ordered a mere thirty minutes into our midday flight. "Can I buy you a drink?"

"What?"

"A drink. See? I've got whiskey now, but I might go full cliché and order wine at thirty thousand feet. Come on, don't tell me you've never sipped wine while crossing the Atlantic."

I shook my head. "No, thanks."

He grinned. "Ah, okay. Tell me if you change your mind though. It's no trouble—makes these long plane rides enjoyable—the drinks and the company."

He did not just say that.

When the plane landed, he stood up, reached into his front pocket, and handed me a business card. He looked down, smiling a little. "Hey—if you ever need help with a project, or business advice, or, I don't know—anything at all . . . give me a call. No pressure. Just . . . life's strange, and people cross paths for weird reasons. Maybe this is one of those."

He pressed the card into my hand and left before I could reply. I grabbed Jeeves from under the seat and waited my turn to deplane.

We ran into each other again at baggage claim. He spotted me across the carousel—and the second he realized I was now seated in a wheelchair, his jaw dropped.

"Sydney! What happened?!" he called out, loud enough to turn a few heads and confuse my wheelchair assistant. Genuine concern was written all over his face, as if he thought I must have taken a tragic tumble somewhere between deboarding and the conveyer belt.

I couldn't help laughing. "I'm disabled," I said. I was tempted to wave his business card at him in a beautiful, graceful threat. *Bet you're glad I'm loyal now, buster.*

When you're heading toward the one you love, there are no charming men but him. And this truth is multiplied a thousand times more when Christ Himself is your Bridegroom. So many of the struggling people I talk to confide in me that they feel their faith can't be real because of their suffering. They have believed something called the "prosperity gospel"—that if they have enough faith in Jesus, God will bless them with riches, health, relationships, and success. This false gospel teaches that worldly prosperity is the result of obedience, and suffering is the result of a lack of faith. If that were true, Jesus Himself would lack the most faith of all—for His suffering was the greatest. Instead, Scripture supports the opposite view: that suffering is the crucible through which God *proves* our faith, through which He *grows* it, *redeems* it, *glorifies* it.

The prosperity gospel flashes its sleek wristwatch, orders whiskey neat from thirty thousand feet, and hands over business cards embossed with gold. But in the face of real suffering, the prosperity gospel collapses like a sandcastle under a rising tide. And that is a problem—because every one of us has suffered, is suffering, or one day will endure real suffering. The gospel of the Bridegroom is that this world is broken, and suffering is part of that brokenness. But rather than collapsing or fleeing in the face of pain, the Bridegroom rushes toward it, sweating drops of blood, bleeding under whips made of animal flesh and metal, bruised and bursting open, nailed to death beams, and displayed naked on a hill for all to see. From the cross He cries:

It is finished!

I have conquered. I have conquered it all.

He rises from the dead. God says: *It is finished indeed.*

Our suffering does not collapse our faith unless our faith was already a house of cards. Rather, our suffering points us to the One who suffered all, so that we may never suffer again. Faith is not believing hard enough to escape the suffering of this life, but receiving with open, undeserving, trusting hands the gift of the Savior to sustain us into the glory of the life to come. We can trust His gift though our hands tremor, spasm, curl, and shake—for His own hands bear the scars of nails.

The Only One

It took twice as long to get out of Germany as I had planned—mostly because the German airport staff forgot about me on the plane terminal and came stalking back an hour later.

"Frau Bennett? Frau Bennett, *ja*?" a tall woman with a stern-looking chin asked me. She held up a sign with my name.

"Yes. *Ja*."

"Frau Bennett. Late!"

She grabbed the handles of my wheelchair and took off with me speeding ahead of her.

"I'm so sorry!" I shouted back, then immediately wondered why *I* was apologizing for being forgotten.

"You go to Mr. Chocolate!" she said.

"Mr. *Who*?" I asked. The way she said it sounded more like Mr. International Gestapo.

She wheeled me up to a large Black man in an airport uniform. "Mr. Chocolate! Mr. Chocolate, *ja*?"

He grabbed the handles of my chair and gave me the first and last smile I ever saw in Germany. "Hi, I'm Mr. Chocolate. The only Black man in this whole airport. And you must be *Frau Bennett*," he added in clear English, despite the thick accent. "I can get you to Poland, or Poznán, or wherever you're going. You just leave it to Mr. Chocolate, *ja*?"

It was the first time I'd felt cared for in hours. I sent up a prayer of thanks right then for Mr. Chocolate.

He pushed me forward. Another airport staffer passed us and gave him the faintest grimace of a smile. "*Herr* Mr. Cho-co-lat," he said.

I could hear the wide, answering smile above my head. "Mr. Chocolate, that's me!" the deep voice exclaimed. "Only Black man you'll see here today. Only chocolate man in this whole German airport."

Mr. Chocolate was, self-proclaimed, the only Black man in the

German airport. He was also the only person there who made me smile, who made me feel safe, who made me feel like I had a friend in foreign territory.

You can wear the things that make you different with shame and self-pity, or you can wear them with dignity and warmth. Realizing you're "the only one"—the only one using a wheelchair, the only one who's been through a divorce, the only one on antidepressants—can often feel like a badge of shame. Or you can tell yourself: *This thing that sets me apart, that makes me different, that everyone notices as soon as they see me—this is the thing I will use to help others.*

Being the "only one" forces you up on a stage beneath a spotlight that can be either terrifying or beautiful. God hands you the microphone and says, "You choose."

Bridegroom

I sat in my wheelchair outside customs in the Poznán International Airport, bulging backpack behind me on my wheelchair handles, luggage at my feet. My mind whirled. *Any minute now.*

I glanced down for the eightieth time at the text Colton had sent me: "On our way. Coming with Sgt. Kusi."

Sergeant Kusi, Colton's squad leader, was a giant of a man from Ghana. I had already met him a few times, but because of Colton's stories, I felt like I'd known him for much longer. He had a big, booming voice, studied every religion, hated the apostle Paul, and had once skinned a goat carcass with a machete in his front yard. When one of the neighborhood boys passed by on his way home from school, Sergeant Kusi lifted the bloody machete out toward him: "Go through my tulip beds again," he growled. He turned his blade and gestured to the goat carcass hanging on the meat hooks, open and disemboweled. I never found out how the boy responded to the threat, but when we went to water Sergeant Kusi's flowers while he was away on a trip, the tulip beds were immaculate.

He had a hard time remembering the name *Sydney*, so he'd resorted to calling me *Australia* instead.

I fidgeted in my chair, checking my reflection in my iPhone screen for the millionth time since landing. My husband of fourteen months hadn't seen me for nearly a year. Was I still how he remembered me? Was I beautiful—even all jet-lagged and exhausted and anxious as I was? What would hugging him be like? Would he smell the same? What if I didn't recognize him somehow?!

The thoughts whirled in my mind. A Polish lady sitting nearby glanced at me and gave me an annoyed grimace. I tried to sit still and failed miserably.

My phone pinged. "Here." I nearly jumped straight up out of my wheelchair. The Polish lady's head shot up.

"Sorry! My husband! Here! Eleven months! Army!" I sputtered, trying to gather my bags. I gave up on the suitcase and kicked it in front of me across the floor.

"Have to go!"

The automatic doors slid open, and I scanned the street. A small rental car pulled up. A large Black man was driving, and there, yes: *him* in the passenger seat. Army uniform, no cap, brown eyes scanning the sidewalk for me.

"Stop!" he shouted. The car slammed to a halt, and its door flew open. In a moment I was off my wheelchair, being lifted, *lifted*, held in my husband's arms, toes trailing across the pavement. His arms were around me. He was strong. And he smelled the same—like Irish Spring original body soap, barracks laundry, and Old Spice deodorant. His nose was buried in my hair, breathing, kissing me. No one was there. No one was in Poland but us.

"Don' *lif* her *up*! Don' *lif* her *up*!" Sergeant Kusi's booming protest sounded behind us. We both laughed softly. Colton put me down.

I clung to his neck, smiling, breathing, as if I had been holding my breath for eleven months. He kissed the top of my head, ran his fingers through my hair, lifted my chin, and looked at me.

"Hi," he whispered.

"Hi," I whispered back.

"Ah, *Australia*! How *awe you doing*?" Sergeant Kusi boomed from behind us. Each syllable was punctuated as if with exclamation marks.

"Be *cahful*, Bennett," he warned as Colton squeezed me against him. "*Be* cahful *with* that *guhl*."

I had fully expected to cry, but I didn't. I couldn't. The tears were weightless. They were up in the sky with the clouds somewhere. They didn't belong on cheeks.

Everything was surreal. Colton, Sergeant Kusi, the deployment, the airports, the ambulance rides, the seizures, the falls, the cane, the wheelchair—everything was surreal. It all was a dream. But Colton's smoothly shaven cheek was pressed against my forehead, and he was kissing me.

"Bennett! Do *no'* squeeze *Australia*!"

We sat in the back seat, holding hands like newlyweds, Sergeant Kusi driving, casting a watchful eye back to us every few seconds in the rearview mirror.

We whispered to each other, breathed each other in. I sank against his strong body, and he put his arm around me. I melted into him and closed my eyes, hearing murmurs of: "*Ah,* Australia. *Australia . . .*" from the front seat.

"How was the trip?" Colton whispered. I thought of the last three days, the layovers, the delayed flights, the trunk of the taxicab, the black cat, the gunshots, the exhaustion, the seizures I had in the airplane bathroom, the tears of complete weakness and exhaustion I shed as I was forgotten in airport after airport, wheeled around by staff, fighting, fighting, fighting to get here, to be in this back seat, riding through Poznán.

I snuggled deeper into him.

"It was perfect," I whispered.

He kissed me. His lips caressed my hair. His voice was soft, an answering whisper, a breath.

"I'm glad."

This whole life—all the suffering, all the joy, all the hope, all the fear—is a trip to our Bridegroom's embrace. Perhaps the whole way through, we will want to scream the word *why* into the darkness above our heads, the ocean of grief that surrounds us, amid the journey we were given and never wanted to have.

Sometimes I can't imagine it, but part of me suspects that when we get there, to the end, the question of *why* will no longer be on our lips. We will know the answer.

To get here. To get here. This is the why for everything.

PART THREE

daughter

THIRTEEN

lines

I was terrified of becoming pregnant until it happened. Then I was in love as soon as the line turned pink. I knelt on the bathroom floor, shaking, sobbing, overwhelmed by the full spectrum of emotions and crying happy, disbelieving tears. Then I wiped my eyes and composed myself, wheeling back into the bedroom where Colton was still in bed.

One month into my trip to Poland, we had received Colton's end date. I began the arduous journey home alone to meet him in Kansas, where Colton would arrive a few days later via Army flight. I flew through Germany again, spent another sketchy night in New York City, and landed back in Manhattan, Kansas, where Larry and Linda—our Bible study leaders whom I hadn't seen in over a year—picked me up from the airport. I was back where the journey had started.

I drove past Grandview Plaza—that inappropriately named apartment complex where Colton and I had spent our first night sleeping on clothes-stuffed pillowcases and an Army sleeping bag; where we had gone dumpster diving for my books; where we were given our first furniture; where I first forgot how to walk, how to speak, how to taste, how to touch. It was the apartment where I first used Jeeves, where I first worried about needing a wheelchair, where I accidentally added too much salt to the ground turkey.

It was June now, the same month in which Colton had left a year ago. The blue Kansas sky stretched above the gray storage compartments that used to be my only view through the curtain-bare window. I could see down the road now into Junction City, and this time, Colton was coming to me.

I spent one last night alone at the Army hotel in Junction City where Colton would be arriving. I dressed myself in the blue flower dress I had bartered for in Poland—through a language barrier, no less. The Polish woman running the underground shop with her daughter had refused to sell me a size she deemed too large for me. She pointed to the dress, opened her arms as wide as she could, and puffed her cheeks out with a word that would be understood in any language: *fat*. Her daughter giggled. Then she pointed to me, squinted her eyes, pursed her lips, and drew her hands in closer than the neck of a wine bottle: *skinny*. She pointed back to the dress and to me again, shaking her head. I didn't know whether to laugh or be insulted.

The day before, an elderly Polish gentleman, excited to show off the little English he knew, explained to Colton and me that I would get to "leave wheelchair" if only I could "lose weight." Poland was confusing. I bought the dress she recommended. Haven't regretted it since.

Now I put the dress on for Colton, twirled in the mirror, posed with Jeeves, makeup just right. I went down to the hotel lobby and waited, glancing at my watch, expecting Army delays as usual. I hitched a ride in a jeep at midnight with a kind sergeant—a windows-down ride that scrambled the hair I had brushed and curled. He unloaded my wheelchair and pointed to a group of people clambering into a warehouse-style building. I pushed myself through the gravel, straining every muscle. The warehouse reeked with bleach and cleaning spray. Men, women, and children lined the bleachers and held homemade signs, smiling, laughing, eyes straining toward the doors that would soon open to their soldiers come home.

I wheeled to the back corner of the room and took my place near the door. A band came out, trumpets blaring. All of us had waited eleven months for this moment. I scanned the faces, having seen Colton just the week before. I had spent most of my time in Poland alone—the strict curfew, travel bans, and weekend drills kept him on post most of the time—but the few hours we had together were worth it. I knew this was supposed to be my first time seeing him in almost a year. This was everyone else's first time seeing their loved ones. They had not had the trial—and blessing—of an arduous international journey, in the unique privacy of a foreign land, intimate conversations guarded by language barriers, seeing where they lived, how they lived, eating, enjoying each other, the mini-honeymoon before the end of the deployment. They had this moment and only this—loud, public, shared with everyone else, with their children, with their friends, with strangers.

The band reached its crescendo with an exultant, eardrum-shattering clamor. People cheered. A loudspeaker boomed over us: "Ladies and gentlemen, the moment you've been waiting for! Time to see your soldiers home! Countdown, please: Ten! Nine! Eight! . . ."

The audience shouted out the numbers with the loudspeaker. Back jean pockets gaped in the spaces above bleachers. Dresses swished up and over knees as women, amid the pure excitement of launching themselves off the bleacher seats the moment their men appeared, surrendered the pristine first impressions they had planned to make.

". . . Two! One! Now, in formation!" Uniformed men, caps on, faces motionless, searching as hard as they could while staring straight ahead, marched into the room through the open doors. The distance between us was pried open by eyes straining to see loved ones. I craned my neck from my wheelchair seat, trying to see through the mass of Army caps, trying to find Colton's profile amid the crowd of army-green camouflage.

A last salute. Parade rest.

"Fall out!"

The sea broke. The organized formation melted into a swarming mass of camouflage embracing sundresses, blue jeans dancing with delight, high heels shrieking across metal bleachers, boots colliding, and tiny tennis shoes pounding over metal seats. I rolled my chair closer, peering through the sea of faces. There were too many people jostling, pushing, trying to do the same thing. I was waist-high, child's height; no one could see me. *Where is Colton? Where is Colton?*

And then I felt strong arms encircle me from behind, a kiss on my cheek, the whisper in my ear answering the question I had never asked out loud: "I'm here."

That was seven months ago. We had moved back to Kansas together, to a better apartment—one with a pool, and furniture, and our own laundry machines. We lived there for four months while Colton finished up his contract, and then he joined the Army Reserve. Then we moved up to Idaho so I could finish my last two years of school. I was a junior now, and Colton worked full-time at the local medical clinic—the same one I had been to so many times while he was gone.

Things were different now when I went in; Colton had found the best personnel for me, people who believed me. I got a custom wheelchair, medication, and consistent medical care. Now it appeared I would need to add an OB to the list. I brushed away the remainder of my tears and grinned. *A baby! A baby!*

I rounded the corner to the room, and there was Colton, waiting for me. I launched myself onto him, wrapping my arms around his neck. He hugged me back, not knowing the cause of my joy but sharing in it just the same.

"Your heart is beating so fast," he said.

My thoughts raced, and I touched the plastic taped to my chest. "You know I need the heart monitor." I grinned. "My heart is always beating fast."

While Colton showered, I drove to the coffee shop, barely containing my excitement. It was our tradition to get coffee together every Saturday morning. "Please," I told the barista, "my husband doesn't know I'm here right now. But when we come in together in a little while, can you write 'You're going to be a dad!' on the lid of his cup?"

She smiled, both of us flushing with excitement. Later, she brought our hot chocolates just as planned: "You're going to be a dad!" and "Congrats!" were scribbled across the black lids with a sparkly gray marker.

Colton stared. "I . . . I think I have the wrong cup," he whispered.

"You don't." I smiled. "We're going to have a baby."

"You—you're pregnant?"

"Yes."

He grabbed my hand and looked at me, eyes wide, eyebrows raised so high they were almost hidden by the hair across his forehead. "Sydney! You're *pregnant*?"

I started laughing. "Yes!"

Still holding my hand, he stared out the window, dazed. "We're going to have a baby?" he asked again, his voice distant.

"We're going to have a baby."

He looked at the coffee cup lid, he looked at mine, and he looked at me. Then he smiled out the window again. I had never seen him so dazed.

"Let's get out of here."

We walked out holding hands. The barista had told some of her family members who were sitting outside on the porch. As we walked out the door, they all cheered. "*Congratulations*!"

"Thank you." I smiled, feeling shy. Colton walked right past as if never seeing them, still holding my hand, still in a dream.

We drove to Lewiston, then up and around the back roads, talking about our brand-new futures.

"Are you scared?"

I put my hand on my belly. "No. I'm not." I was a mother already, protective and in love with the tiny human inside me. I felt at peace and calm—calm enough to reassure Colton, the steady one, who was as scattered as seeds before the wind.

"I'm a dad! I'm a dad! I'm a *dad*!" he kept saying over and over, as if trying to make himself believe it, trying to grasp the reality he didn't know would face him over his cup of hot chocolate that morning. I watched him, enjoying the sight of him going through the full rush of emotions I had just been through a couple hours before.

"We need a car seat—we need outlet covers!"

I laughed.

"It's not funny. I'm being serious! Take out your phone and write it down right now."

I dutifully typed: *Car seat. Outlet covers.* "Anything else?"

He thought for a moment. "Crib?"

Crib.

Tomb

Four weeks later, the line was not pink, but red—blood, as my uterus became a tomb for my baby. I didn't expect miscarriage to feel like labor with severe contractions and pain. I didn't expect my body to feel so empty. I didn't expect so much love and grief for someone I knew for so short a time. My body felt pummeled and bruised in the midst of my devastation. Death was passing through me. I was a mother without a baby, and I felt the hollow ache of that truth in my cramping stomach and my weeping heart.

"Your baby died two weeks ago," the doctor told us. "It's only measuring at six weeks. Your body just didn't know."

The doctor said "your body," but I heard "you." *You didn't know.* And how could I not have known? The love, the connection, the instant *oneness* I felt with this child who was as much a part of me as it was its own image-bearer—was it all an illusion, make-believe, not real love?

This baby had been a joy. A gift. A blessing conceived in a body already broken by pain and loss. A way God had asked for our trust again, one more time—not with a fresh grief but with a fresh joy we were not ready for. A way God was saying to us: *I love you. I see your pain. And I have not forgotten you.*

This new child I loved with an aching heart, but there was no less *love* because of the ache. And God was gracious to work against my fears. Oh, so gracious.

Then the strange signs. The blood on the towel. The new kind of pain. The ultrasound.

No heartbeat.

Why?

Why in my body of brokenness and pain would God give new glory, only to take it away? Why would God put such fresh love in a heart full of old grief, to break it again, sorrow upon sorrow? Why would God create a victory within this failing brokenness, to have the victory lost in failure? Why did it seem God was alighting my hopes with another dream, then crushing the tentative fingers that reached out to hold it?

"I should have known. *I should have known,*" I sobbed to the other mama on the phone. She was older than me, wiser. We'd never met in person, but she had had ten miscarriages—so she knew. "It makes me feel like nothing I felt for my baby was real."

"It *was* real," she said. "It was so real that your body fought *that hard*, for *two weeks*, to keep your baby, even when it was already too late. That's how real it was."

"My baby was dead inside me for two weeks. I was a tomb and didn't even know it."

"No, you're not a tomb. You're a mother. And even those two weeks were a gift. You had the gift of holding your baby for all those days, even when its heart had stopped beating. What a beautiful thing that is. What a beautiful, sacrificial love that is."

"Colton wants me to take something for the pain. But I don't want to. I want to hurt."

"I know," she whispered. "It's okay. Your baby died. It's supposed to hurt."

Empty

I lay in bed, pain all over, frantic between seizures. Crying, sobbing—I didn't know what was happening. Colton lay beside me, arms over my chest to keep me down in the bed where I was safe, but I didn't understand what he was saying. I kept trying to get up. I groped at my belly, cramping, tight with pain. *Something is wrong.*

"My tummy feels empty! My tummy feels empty!"

"I know," Colton said, gripping my hands, squeezing them tightly, kissing my wet cheeks, and moving away the hair plastered to my forehead.

"Where is the baby?"

His voice broke. "Darling . . . the baby died."

I screamed. I screamed my grief and pain from the bottom rung of my stomach. The scream erupted into sobs. And then, a whimper: *"I want it back."*

The episode lasted an hour. Three seizures later, I woke up. Colton still held me. I didn't remember what had happened, but my cheeks were still wet with tears, my body still hurting.

"Are you okay?" Colton asked. His voice was quiet.

I nodded.

"Go to sleep, baby. It's okay."

I rolled over, exhausted. He stayed next to me until my breathing slowed. Then he left the room and sat in a chair at the dining table. He stared blankly. He prayed. He was there for two hours, remembering the baby, remembering the scream.

Colton didn't tell me about that night until days afterward. I was still walking hunched over, sore and bruised, aching in my heart and my womb. For three years, I had learned to grieve an exposed brokenness—an external disability that was obvious, apparent to anyone who looked at me. Now I was learning to grieve something invisible, something no one had ever seen. A fresh crack splintered my already broken heart. New tears filled my already full bottle. Another ache settled in my already aching soul.

But one day, no more.

One day your heart—shielded by your Savior—will be made new, and beat in a glorified chest. One day God will collect your last tear and say, "It is finished," then set the cork in that tear-filled bottle as you walk through heaven's gates. One day the ache and sorrow of *missing* will be replaced with the joy of *seeing*.

Maybe today.

Maybe tomorrow.

Maybe decades of aches and tears, many bottles from now.

But for that day, we wait. *Come, Lord Jesus. Come!*

Resurrection

Colton lay next to me in bed, typing on the laptop. The keys went quiet. I didn't look up.

The grief over my physical brokenness had been devastating. Earth-shattering. Crushing. Some days, it still is. It is possible that nothing will heal my constant physical pain until glory. But even in some of my darkest moments, I have still seen slivers of what God was doing through it all. I have seen the ripples of His work through my pain and brokenness, touching people's lives in ways I could only begin to understand.

But this new death—this miscarriage—felt so . . . different. It felt senseless. This baby had been a comfort. A way of God saying: *I love you. I haven't forgotten you. Here. You've walked through pain and sorrow, and I know it's still there, but here's a fresh salve, a fresh love. Here's new life; here's another joy and future.*

And my heart, without knowing it, had been so ready for this new love. So *ready*, and anxious, and full of longing—feeling such a confused myriad of joys and sorrows and hopes all at once.

But God snuffed it out. No heartbeat.

"Hey," Colton said from beside me, pulling my thoughts back to the present. "You can be sad. But you have to be sad in the right way."

I turned and looked at him. "I know. I just . . . I am *so sad*."

"Me too."

I knew in that moment, as I took my brokenness, my anger, my sorrow, and held them up to heaven with open hands, I knew God was still good. But what was He doing? None of this made sense. I already thought my body long past the breaking point, but this was not just another wave of the same old grief. It was a brand-new sorrow.

By the time I gave birth, there was no recognizable baby. Death had passed through me, and so had the decomposition of death. Miscarriage and stillbirth: the only times it is possible for a human being to literally taste death within their body—and not die. I cried at the sight of formless blood and tissue tangled in the lifeless amniotic sac. And I flushed the toilet.

Jesus wept at the grave of Lazarus. He wept at the side of a dead body He knew He would make alive again. And yet He wept. He wept because death is tragic. Death is terrible. Death is wrong. He wept because death screams out in one final, ghastly cry that this world is broken and cursed.

It is good to weep at what is wrong with the world. It is good to weep when your soul is screaming: *This isn't the way it is supposed to be.* It is good to weep with loss, with pain, with the unshakable burden of grief. It is good to weep when the weight of sorrow seems to suffocate any possibility of life or wonder ever breathing again in your soul. It is good to weep with Jesus.

Death is an enemy. Death is real. Death is a sign the story is not over yet.

When I was pregnant, I woke up every morning thinking of my baby. It was there, in my mind, in my body—present, felt, when I wheeled my chair around the kitchen for breakfast, drove to class, took notes during the lecture. No one there knew of this little life inside me. No one but me. It was my tiny, happy little secret deep inside, the ever-present catalyst of my growing love and trust and happiness. I never stopped thinking about my baby.

Even when it died.

Because when I woke up the next morning, in the place of the seed I felt inside me, I sensed an empty, shredded womb. Where the presence had been, there was only brutality and ache. I felt emptiness in me wherever I went, where I used to feel my baby.

There is a saturating gluttony in grief. Grief steals whatever it finds. It feeds on every part of you. It not only makes you think you'll never be full again but also makes you feel you don't even *want* to be. How can you be happy when you're still in this part of the story? How can you be happy before the story God is writing is over and He lifts your broken body off the ground, presses the cork into your precious bottle of tears, smiles, and says: "It is finished"?

God is still showing that to me. But ultimately, the answer lies in the fact that *such a day is coming*. One day, this will end. Think about that. Let it seep into every aching joint, every cancerous cell, every screaming breath, every pang of guilt, every agony of sorrow, every anguish of loss, every stab of memory, every weight of sin, every pound of shame, every cry of the soul. *One day, this will end.*

We serve a God who has endured death, suffered death, conquered death. We serve a God who knows what it is to cry in pain, to suffer physically, to bear anguish undeserved, to have death pass through Him. We serve a God who weeps. We serve a God who lives. We serve a God who is victorious in a world that seems to offer only pain and defeat.

Death's heartbeats in the aching womb of this world are numbered. His end is sure. And there will be no sorrow at his passing. No emptiness. There will be fullness, joy, and glory forevermore. The birth pangs will not bring forth fresh sorrow but fresh life. As they are meant to. As they were always meant to.

I turned to Colton beneath the covers, looked at him, my cheeks dry, my body heavy with grief.

"I don't want to celebrate my birthday next week. It feels so wrong. Our baby will never have a birthday."

He kissed me. "Our baby will have a resurrection day. And that is better."

FOURTEEN

strength

When the gift came again, I was ready. I knew before it was possible to know—before the pink line, before any symptoms. I *knew.* I hadn't been ready to be pregnant before. I hadn't been ready for the uncertainty, the physical strength needed in a body already so weak. But I hadn't counted on one thing: How could I? I didn't know the mother's love that would do *anything* for her child. And suddenly, there I was, in my wheelchair, uncertainty looming as prominently as my growing belly.

"What's the scariest part of pregnancy with a disability?" someone asked me.

"The next part."

It was true. Before my pregnancy, I wondered how my body would cope with the fatigue and morning sickness of the first trimester. It properly floored me, but when it happened, I was busy wondering how my body would handle the added weight and growing belly in the next trimester. Then, how I would cope with the pain of labor. Then the sleep deprivation of the newborn stage. Each time I reached a new point,

I started getting anxious about the part coming next—not realizing I was living the thing I had been afraid of just a little while earlier.

And isn't that always how it is? With chronic pain, disability, or any long struggle, we're constantly looking ahead to the next challenge, bracing ourselves for the next potential wave of hardship. We worry about how we'll cope if things get worse, how we'll manage if we lose more strength, if the pain increases, if independence slips further away. But in doing so, we don't see that we're already enduring what we once thought we couldn't. Months or even years ago, the version of yourself who feared today didn't know how God would strengthen you through it. You couldn't see the ways you would learn to adapt, to rest, to fight, to laugh, to love and be loved.

God's strength is in the present, not the future. But don't worry; the future will be the present one day. When you get there, He will be there too. It was a gift when God made me realize—with the faint hint of a joke—the insane cycle I was creating for myself. I laughed and said, "How silly," and the anxiety eased after that.

Physically, however, pregnancy did not get easier. My wheelchair use shifted from 70 percent to 95 percent of the day. I was in pain all the time; not just my normal pain, but the pain of weight, ligaments, and muscles stretching over bones that were tearing apart. Every time the pain started getting to me, I thought of our first baby. Each ache, each searing nerve, each added pound, each change to my skin, my broken frame, my fragile heart, was a gift—a gift I knew was precious, for it had once been taken from me.

My labor was fifty-two hours long. When it was time to push, I lay seizing in the hospital bed. Seizure. Push. Seizure again.

"I don't have the strength," I whispered, my body limp, spent. "The seizures . . . they're . . . they're taking everything."

"You have to." The OB grabbed my foot and squeezed. "You can do this. Let the seizures come, then push in between them."

God, You have to do this for me, I prayed in my mind. *God, help me!*

Motherhood

We named her Hadassah. The Hebrew name of Esther in the Bible. A woman of strength, of courage, of grief, of beauty.

I'm a disabled mom. But when I pick up my sweet daughter, when I roll down the sidewalk with her strapped close to my heart, when I lay her on my lap and sing her songs around the house, when I rock her back and forth, wheel her in my arms to the bed, and lay her down to sleep—when I see her big, wondering eyes looking up into mine, when I kiss her sleepy smiles, her long fingers, her little toes, when I clean the spit-up, change messy diapers, navigate sleep schedules, wake windows, leaking breast milk, and outfit changes—when I soothe her cries, wake up every three hours, all night and all day, to sleepily fight away sleep and tend to her needs—when I thank her for being my baby girl and tell her I love being her mama—when my heart aches with love so much it hurts, and she warms my whole soul and more, and when I understand that here I am, in the most natural and the most foreign place in the world, as brand-new as my baby, that's when I know I'm not a disabled mom—but a mom—and it surprises me each time in all its glorious simplicity.

God did not make a mistake when He made me like this. He did not miscalculate when He wrote my story, weaving together my life, Colton's, and Hadassah's in a way that only He could. From the beginning, He ordained that I would be her mother and she would be my daughter. He ordained that my hands—whether carrying her, soothing her, or guiding my wheelchair through tremors—would be enough through Him.

The world measures motherhood in strength, stamina, energy, and organizational skills. God measures it in love, in faithfulness, in the willingness to pour yourself out for the sake of another. By the world's measure, I should not be a mother. By God's measure, I am the only mother He *chose* for my baby.

It is not only in parenthood you may wonder if you are enough.

The world may pass the verdict that you are lacking—that your body or circumstances disqualify you from living the life God has given you. Here is the truth: You *are* lacking. But here is the good news: God only chooses those who are lacking to fill with His strength. Your story and your struggles are not proof of failure; they are proof of purpose. Proof of His perfect storytelling skills. Proof of His beautiful plan amid the chaos, and pain, and mayhem that is this life.

When I look at Scripture, I don't see God working through strong, capable, able-bodied mothers who have everything in order. I see God working through Eve, who incited sin and bore a murderer (Genesis 3–4); through Sarah, old and barren (Genesis 11–22); through Hagar, the cast-out bondwoman (Genesis 16); through Leah, the unloved and unbeautiful (Genesis 29–31, 35, 49; Ruth 4). I see God working through the mother of Moses, Jochebed, who faithfully kept and saved her baby when his future seemed impossible (Exodus 2:1–10; Numbers 26:59). I think of Hannah weeping for a child and praying so fervently the priest thought she was drunk (1 Samuel 1–2). Of Mary, the virgin, the unmarried center of scandal, tasked with raising the Son of God (Luke 1–2).

And I see Jesus—the Savior of the world—choosing to embody weakness, to be born into poverty, to live a life of suffering from feeding trough to death beam. The Strong not only rescuing the weak but *choosing* to be one of them. God has never been in the business of choosing the strong ones. He is in the business of showing His strength through the ones who know their desperate need of Him.

People stare. Argue eugenics in the comment section of my social media. Debate whether I should have had my baby. Other moms don't see the word *abortion* in their online birth announcements, or have their genetics dissected by strangers deciding whether those genes were good enough to pass on. The world—dicing up parenthood into body parts and working arms and legs, so concerned that my wheelchair makes me a bad mom—doesn't understand yet what it means to be one.

Hadassah is one year old now. I sometimes forget how different we look to the world, because at home we just feel like us.

Surrender

"I can't feel anything that touches my arms or legs," I told Colton one afternoon at the dining table in Kansas, back when we were first married. I had been sick for two weeks, and every new symptom devastated me. My eyes filled with tears. "It makes me feel so alone."

He leaned over, took my cold, curled-in hands in his warm, steady ones, and looked at me.

He kissed my cheek. "Can you feel this?" he whispered. He kissed me again. "And this? And this?"

He brushed my tears with his finger. "You're not alone."

Now when I lose feeling, I am not devastated. I wake up from a seizure and tell Colton, "I can't feel the whole right side of my body."

"The right side?" he laughs. "That's so random."

I giggle.

"Want me to help you get it back?"

"Yes, please."

He nods, pulls off the blanket, and picks up my legs—stiff, ice-cold, locked in spasm. "Think as if you're helping me," he says.

I'm not doing any of the work at first; he's the one moving my leg up and down as I lie flat on my back, my body convulsing and shaking as my brain fights for control once more. When I've regained some connection, enough to feel the pain: "Do you want to try to walk?"

"Yes."

He lowers my legs off the bed for me and stands up, wrapping my arms around his neck. I cling to him, legs wobbling. He inches backward, and I twist and drag my feet after us like blocks of wood.

I'm not the one moving my legs at first; Colton is. I'm not the one holding myself up; his arms keep me from falling. My job isn't to will myself into motion, to force my body to do the work it cannot do. My job is to act in faith—that my feeble obedience will be met by Colton's strength.

So often, we think of faith as effort—as God calling us to muscle through, to prove our strength, to show we are capable of standing on our own. But faith isn't about forcing what you cannot control. It is about yielding to the One who controls all things. It is about letting Christ do the work you cannot do yourself.

Colton doesn't push my body beyond what he can bear, but he does ask me to move before I am ready. And then—he moves for me. He lifts me. He pulls me close when I wobble and begin to fall. Jesus carries the weight you cannot bear. Real strength—strength in the Lord—is not about building muscle but building dependence. Real strength is knowing on whom to lean. For "the LORD will fight for you; you need only to be still" (Exodus 14:4 NIV).

"How many days on your count right now?" Colton asks. He knows I count the days I've had since a fall.

"Eighty-two," I exclaim. My legs buckle, and he pulls me in tight against him.

"Nope," he says. "I'm not letting you reset that thing tonight."

When the spasms return to my legs, we know it's enough.

"You're beautiful right now."

I look up, nightgown disheveled, hair falling into my face, legs twisted underneath me, tremoring with silent convulsions as I cling to him, my arms around his neck for support.

"Thank you."

"Can I go to bed now?"

I laugh. "Yes—thank you for helping me."

"Always, princess."

FIFTEEN

lessons

I gripped the microphone and smiled at the sea of students and faculty below me. April, the talent show performance at New Saint Andrews College—my first and last before graduation. Tonight, Hadassah had her first babysitter. Colton, who carried my wheelchair onto the stage, now took his seat, watching me with easy confidence, waiting.

"My legs don't work well," I began. "I don't know why I'm trying stand-up."

I deliberately stepped on the laughter of my first joke: "People are always a bit unsure if they're allowed to laugh when I make jokes about my disability. You are, and I hope you do—because that will increase my chances of winning."

The room relaxed with a chuckle, and I relaxed with them. Since I had to sit in a wheelchair to give this speech, you could bet I intended to have fun with it.

"Let me start by telling you a bit about my disability. I have functional neurological disorder, or FND, which means my brain doesn't communicate correctly with my central nervous system."

There. The diagnosis I once tried so hard to hide. Little did I know, someone else in the audience had recently been diagnosed with FND as well. She sat watching, seeing humor triumph four years further down the road she traveled.

"People don't know what causes this yet, but we do know symptoms can be exacerbated by stress. So I came to NSA."

The audience laughed now. Nearly every student at New Saint Andrews had chosen the school for its academic rigor, embracing the challenge. The strong education came with a *relentless* undercurrent of stress, certainly not ideal for my disorder—but I loved it.

I thought back to my sophomore year, when I struggled through biology and anatomy. I was often leaving the room to have seizures on the bathroom floor, whispering the Calvin–Benson cycle through convulsions on my mattress.

"I took Dr. Wilson's biology course to find out how my body *doesn't* work." I smiled. "It was basically a whole year of: *Ohhhh . . .* That's *what it's supposed to do.*"

Most of my college experience hadn't been defined by learning new things—although that came in abundance—but by relearning the old things. How to speak. How to breathe through convulsions. How to orient myself after a seizure alone.

"Having a brain and nervous system disorder can cause just about any symptom in the book."

Many people talk about "visible" versus "invisible" disability. Visible disability can be seen through obvious malformation and is often accompanied by a mobility aid of some sort. Invisible disability can't be easily seen from the outside—conditions such as brain trauma, epilepsy, multiple sclerosis, and yes, often, FND. After living with my own illness for so many years and becoming part of a community of many other chronic illness sufferers, I've become convinced that seldom is a disability truly "invisible." Suffering is almost always there if you look closely enough—the weariness behind the eyes, the droop of the shoulders, the slowness or jerkiness about the movements, the canceled plans, the difficulty tracking conversation. We just don't often look closely enough to see each other's pain.

"In the first two weeks of becoming sick, I lost the ability to walk, speak, taste, and move my arms and legs. Seizures started. Hallucinations too."

I remembered one time I clawed my way back to speaking—just to the point of painful, stuttering, slurring communication—only to have another seizure and lose it all again. I remembered the despair I felt, the frustration, anger, and hopelessness that filled my chest. Colton, ever patient, had pulled out a book once more and sat down beside me. I looked at him as if he were insane. *Listen to your body*, people have grown fond of saying. Well, what do you do if your body is screaming, "Give up! Give up!"?

"The first time I lost the ability to speak, it lasted three days. The third day was Easter Sunday, and I didn't want to go to church.

"I thought: It's going to be so awkward. People will come up and talk to me, and I'll just have to sit there. Like, what am I supposed to do? That's so uncomfortable!

"I typed all this on my phone to Colton, and he says: 'That's not a good enough reason to skip church.'

"So we went. And that's when I realized how much of an introvert I am—because no one noticed.

"They were just like: 'Oh, yeah, that's Sydney. She . . . doesn't talk.'"

Every time I had to relearn, Colton had to reteach me. He, too, had to go over each letter and word, over and over. He had to listen to my stuttering, halting sentences—sentences he could have read ten times over by the time I was done.

B . . . ba-ba-ba.

C . . . ca-ca-ca.

"The timeline of getting sick was a bit hectic. We got married, then two weeks later I became disabled—literally overnight. My symptoms started with sudden hand paralysis while driving home from a date night . . . Yeah, I'm thinking of leaving that restaurant a review on Yelp."

This marriage. This life. Disabled two weeks after our honeymoon. Separated for eleven out of the first fourteen months of our marriage. Our baby—the miscarriage—Hadassah. It all meant something. I looked back now, and I could see—through the pain, the laughter, the loneliness, and despair—it all mattered.

It's hard to see what matters in the moments when your pain feels meaningless. God can see the whole tapestry at once, but we can only see a few tangled threads in the midst of it. You need time to see the finished woven row—maybe just a few inches of meaning—in this life. But often, that is enough to give you hope. One day, you'll see the tapestry as God does. Meaning will be applied to every single thread. It all will matter. It already does.

"A month later, I was diagnosed. Three months after that, Colton deployed overseas, and I came back for my sophomore year at NSA. While he was gone, I had to call the ambulance twice. The first time was funny because I was on the third floor, and the EMTs forgot the stretcher. So I was lying on the floor, totally out of it, as they argued about the best way to get me downstairs. They settled on carrying me down in the big fluffy brown blanket from my bed. When I got down to the ambulance, this seasoned paramedic was waiting and he said, 'You scared all my EMTs.' I was like, 'Sir, did you see that stairwell? They were scaring *me*.'"

No matter how many times a seizure or a fall happened, the floor always felt foreign. But the sorrow? The sorrow was familiar. It lingered in my heart long before disease inhabited my body. It is facing *that* sorrow, that ache, that turmoil of spirit, and bringing all *that* brokenness to the foot of the cross—that is the lesson we must really learn again and again.

"The second time, I had trouble breathing. Called 911. Dispatch asked if I could speak any louder.

"I was like: 'No, sorry. Can't talk louder right now.'

"'Ma'am, are you unable to speak louder because there's a threat in the room?'

"'No.'

"'Ma'am, who else is in the room with you?'

"'No one.'

"'Ma'am, is someone else in the room?'

"'No.'

"So obviously she concludes there's a threat in the room. Sends a police officer to my apartment first."

I have fallen into depression and doubt more often than I have fallen on the floor. I wrestled with shame far longer than I did with the humiliation of my symptoms. I cried out to the Lord from a place of desperation that long predated physical suffering. Anxiety dogged me before I lived alone. I lacked control of my life and future before disability ever made me so keenly aware of the fact. I battled pride long before I struggled for dignity.

"The police officer's banging on the door, and I'm literally crawling over to let him in because he says if I don't open it for him, he's going to bust the door down. (We were renting.) I kinda pull myself up against the wall, open the door—then he comes in and asks if I'm okay.

"I'm like: 'Yeah, I'm okay,' and start to fall down.

"He jumps forward and catches me and holds me up and—this is how I know my sense of humor is broken, because the first thought that ran through my mind as he's holding me is: *Now I can tell people that I've been caught and held by the police.*"

That call. That call that led to the terrifying hospital visit. Not being believed. Catheters threatened. Exposed on the toilet. Eye rolls.

The taxi drive home, paid with a smile. There was laughter behind that story now. Laughter is sometimes the greatest proof of redemption we can present in this life.

"That police officer ended up being the one to call the paramedics. And apparently, my story had been making its rounds through the fire department and the police department because six months after the first call, all he did was pull up his radio and say, 'Yeah, I'm with her right now. It's the same thing as last time.'

"*The same thing as last time!* It was like when you go to a restaurant so often that they know your order. Except this was my ambulance order: 'Yes, 911? I'll take my usual. Yeah. Stretcher on the side, please.'"

Through death, through suffering, through loss, through grief, through pain, God reteaches us lessons He has taught all our lives, bringing us back to battles we need to fight over and over.

"You do get a lot of weird questions with a disability. This one time, I went to the doctor for pain medication, and they always want to see where you are with diet and exercise before prescribing anything.

"So I remember he asked me—completely serious, he asked me this—'Have you tried running?'

"I was like, 'Yes, I have. That's the problem.'"

Now, I had relearned the same lessons my daughter would learn for the first time—how to speak, how to walk, how to laugh, get out of bed, be a person. How many children watch their parents learning to speak or walk alongside them? How many see their parents experiencing the vulnerability of learning something everyone already knows? But it's not just me. We all have to relearn things all the time. We have to take the same lessons over and over.

"People always ask, 'What happened to you?' 'What's wrong with you?' 'Why are you in a wheelchair?' It's gotten to the point where it's more fun just to make something up.

"So one time, I walked past Mingles, and this guy was standing out in front, a bit intoxicated, and he shouted out at me as I went by: 'Are you recovering?'

"So I said, 'Yes, I am recovering!'

"He asked, 'Oh, man—what are you recovering from?'

"I said, 'I was shot. While stopping a bank robbery.'

"He was completely taken aback and started stammering, 'A-at what bank?!'

"Okay, that was a fair question. I didn't know what to say, so I said, 'Oh, gosh, I'm new to the area—what's the bank that you use?'

"He said, 'Such-and-such bank?'

"I said, 'Yes! That's the one!'

"He looked so completely horrified. But if you're worried about this poor man, don't be. I was quick to reassure him—that I was successful."

C. S. Lewis wrote that "relying on God has to begin all over again every day as if nothing had yet been done."[1] Getting out of bed is new every morning. The battle carries on, as long as we inhale oxygen.

Maybe you feel as if you are stuck in the same place. Maybe depression is pulling you into a pit you hoped never to enter again. Maybe old memories you thought healed are reawakening. Maybe relationships you thought reconciled are tearing apart—a painful anniversary is bringing back sorrow, a persistent sin you've long battled is haunting you with new strength. Or maybe every day feels like a slow repeat of the day before—the same feeling of dread when you open your eyes, the same tasks again and again, long work hours, diaper changes, exhaustion, boredom, drudgery, dishes, laundry, messy rooms. Go to sleep. Begin again.

"People think my disability is sad . . ."

It's easy to think you should be further along in this fight than you feel right now. That you should have overcome this. That you should no longer be struggling the way you are.

". . . but I have a great life."

Perhaps the battle you are seeing as a sign of your lack of faith is the very thing God is using to prove your faith in Him.

"God is so good that He gives us not only joy through our sufferings, but even laughter."

True faith is not demeaning our awareness of pain but being so acutely aware of the *wrongness* of that pain that we must turn to God and fix our thoughts on glory. Heaven is meaningless to those who have not grieved. Pain awakens us so that even with eyes filled with tears, our hearts cry to God and say: "One day, this wrongness will end. But not yet. Not yet."

"One of my symptoms is called gait ataxia. It causes my legs to spasm out to the side when I walk."

Faith. Not the muting of lament, but the carrying of that lament to the throne of God. Not the suppression of sadness, but the lifting high of our sadness for the Lord to see. Not the denial of pain but knowing this pain will one day be turned to glory. Not the abjuration of sorrow but the knowledge we serve a Lord acquainted with sorrow. Not claiming victory in our futile attempts at holiness but knowing that in Christ, victory has already been claimed.

"Whenever people say I must be sad because I'm disabled, I just show them this . . ."

I rose from my chair, cane and microphone dangling from my hands. Each step an exhausting, ludicrous effort.

Lift leg. Spasm out to the side. Balance. Hover. Lower leg. Lift.

People laughed at the sight. I displayed my disability onstage for them all to see. I smiled at the laughter—I felt it too: the humor of this brokenness.

The goal of our trust in God is not to turn us into stoics. It is not to numb our hearts to grief, loss, or sorrow. The Christian, above all, has most reason to be profoundly affected by suffering. We know the way it's supposed to be. The road to salvation has always begun in crucifixion. Those who weep are perhaps closest to the Savior, who also wept on His way to redeem every tear.

Years ago, I hadn't wanted anyone to see my legs like this—to see my brokenness, my vulnerability. Now I teetered on the edge of a stage, my shattered pieces glued together with flecks of gold. Somehow God refined my inelegance, dignified my clumsy steps, brought me a smile at the end of months of pain and tears.

We rest in the promise that as we are brought to what may seem like the same fight—the same battle, the same pain and toil and chaos again and again—the suffering we feel acknowledges the truth of the brokenness in this world. A brokenness that will one day be redeemed.

I grinned at the crowd—exposing my worst fear: being human before humans. My flapping legs stilled, tremoring beneath me. Faithful Jeeves planted on the floor.

"Because that, my friends," I said, looking out at the laughing faces, "that's called walking with a spring in your step."

SIXTEEN

walk

I sat on the floor with my newborn in my arms, trying to breathe. My wheelchair was only a few feet away. Moments before, I had been sitting in it when the familiar warning signs of a seizure aura and onsetting paralysis began. It was my first full day alone with my baby. I was still recovering from COVID-19—which, in a yet-unknown, under-researched way, seems to amplify the symptoms of certain neurological conditions. I knew that staying in my wheelchair any longer would put me at risk of a fall as my symptoms worsened.

Careful not to wake Hadassah, I locked the brakes and lowered myself to the floor, one hand gripping the wheelchair frame, the other cradling her small, sleeping body against my chest. I had rehearsed this scenario in my mind many times. It was bound to happen soon—especially with the added strain of illness on top of postpartum recovery. I let out my breath slowly.

I didn't panic. I had a baby now. I wasn't allowed to panic.

Leaning back against the wall, I looked down at the sleeping baby in my arms. She hadn't stirred. Her tiny eyelids remained closed, long lashes resting against soft, full cheeks. She was only a few weeks old. Every precaution I took for myself was also for her—ensuring I would be able to care for her, no matter how my symptoms worsened. I pulled my phone closer and opened my call history, ready to dial Colton if needed. He would be able to stay on the line with me and send an ambulance if necessary. He knew my symptoms almost as well as I did now. He wouldn't panic either. We had planned for this.

The tremors started—slow at first, then intensifying. My muscles grew rigid, painful, spastic. I adjusted Hadassah, resting my arms between my legs to steady them and support her head. I maneuvered myself farther into the corner, braced my body against the kitchen cabinets, ensured she was supported, and waited.

The seizure passed. Easily. I knew that it would.

I remained on the floor until my spastic muscles relaxed enough to be able to bend my knees. I scanned the room for a safe place to set Hadassah down while I worked to regain control of my muscles. Normally, Colton helped me with this part. Today, I was alone.

I spotted her swing across the room. *That will work.*

Scooting across the floor, I held her against my chest with my one free arm, resting when I needed to, head between my knees, slowing my breath, steadying my heart. Pushing my phone a few feet ahead and then scooting to meet it—the same way I had done so long ago, on my studio floor while Colton was deployed. But I wasn't afraid this time. The next steps seemed obvious: *Get to the swing. Put the baby down. Learn to walk again.*

When I reached the swing, Hadassah stirred for the first time. I set her inside, turned on the vibration, and watched as she settled.

Steps one and two: *Done.*

I scooted a few feet farther in the direction of the couch, gripped the sides, and wrangled myself up onto my knees. I leaned back, testing my weight against my numb, tingling legs, coaxing awake the muscles that were so tight and inoperable. After a few seconds, I twisted my body up again—then down, then up—bracing my arms against the couch, lifting, lowering, resting, repeating.

"Think as if you're helping me," I whispered to my legs—the same words Colton always whispered to me. It was my reminder not to force the movement before it was ready. The parts of my body were separate right now, and that was okay. At first, my arms were doing all the work—pulling my body up, bracing my weight against the couch, lowering myself with control again.

The aching pain returned—a good sign. I still wouldn't try to walk, not yet. First, I had to get Hadassah to bed. If I paced myself, I had a chance of holding on to this fragile progress without slipping into a seizure and starting the process over again.

I didn't expect my first medical episode alone to happen while holding my newborn—but I knew this was a possibility. What I hadn't guessed was that it would take place while Colton was five hours away in Boise, and while I was recovering from my second round of coronavirus. But anxiety, fear, panic—those luxuries belonged to a different version of me: the childless Sydney, the newly disabled woman, the one still learning how to navigate marriage and life from a wheelchair.

But not now.

Now I had a child. I had one option: Plan for the medical episodes to happen.

Then do the next right thing.

Fighting

Having a child taught me one thing early on—something I'm not sure I could have learned as deeply any other way: I had more control over my reactions to fear than I ever believed. Ever since becoming disabled, I'd felt powerless—not only over my circumstances but also over myself. My mind and body fought against me, distorting reality, making the correct, steady, logical actions feel foreign, if not impossible. Now, when depression weighed heavy on me in the mornings, staying in bed was no longer an option. I had to get up. I had to eat. I had to shower, take my medication, care for myself—not just for me, but for her. I couldn't let myself spiral, no matter how irresistibly my body and mind seemed to tug me in that direction. I couldn't give in to whatever grief, or anxiety, or fatigue, or pain *wanted* me to do. I needed to do what my baby needed me to do. My next step had already been decided; I only needed to step into it faithfully.

A few nights after Hadassah was born, after I had been awake for seventy-two hours, my body reached a physical breaking point. I had seizures over and over, back-to-back. I could no longer hold my own baby. I struggled to roll over, tapped Colton awake, and managed one word—"Help"—before the next seizure took me under.

Colton grabbed the crying baby and held my hand, trying to take care of both of us, turning his attention first to one and then the other. When I woke, I couldn't move. Pain, exhaustion, hormones, and sheer depletion had caught up to me. The moment I realized my helplessness, I broke.

"I don't know if I can do this," I sobbed. "I can't sleep—and when I do, I've been having nightmares again. I can't move my arms or legs right now. I can't figure out breastfeeding—it hurts so much, and I can't keep her awake long enough to eat. I feel like I'm forcing both of us to push through something we don't have the strength for. And I can't get a break. And I'm so, *so tired*. What if I'm getting worse? What if I never get a break? It's all coming down so hard, all at once, and I don't know what to do."

Colton put his finger to my lips, quieting me. He put his hand under my chin and turned my head up to look at him.

"No, Sydney," he said, his voice gentle, steady. "You can't do that. You can't go back there. Okay?"

I looked at him, teary-eyed, confused.

He took my hand and placed it on Hadassah's tiny chest, which rose and fell in a fitful sleep. "Look at her," he said. "Look at our little girl. You can't go back there. That girl I knew when we were first married? Uh-uh. You can't do that again. You can't let yourself. You need to be strong for Hadassah. You need to do the right thing by her."

He squeezed my hand. "I will help you, okay? I will help you. You're not alone in this. But you have to do your part. That means you can't take the easy way out. You can't let yourself spiral, even when your mind and body want to. You need to hold on tight to the truth of what you know. You need to fight—because you're fighting for her now."

He lifted Hadassah up to my limp, motionless arms, then held her against me. "You're fighting for *her*."

I nodded. That was the first and only time I allowed myself to panic after she was born. The hard days haven't ended—there are many. Days I need help. Days when symptoms take over my body or mind, when I am scared, incoherent, or confused. Some days, all I can do is sink, but if I sink let it be in God's water. "Look at that little sleeping baby there. Look at our daughter," Colton had said. So I look at my baby. And I pray to God. Shifting my gaze back and forth between the two, holding, being carried.

School

I pulled into the handicap space and shifted the car into park. Outside, the mid-January snow stood in uneven heaps along the sidewalk. I had delivered Hadassah amid the biggest snowstorm of the year, while the outside temperature was in the negative teens and snow fell in piles from the skies. We took her home in exactly zero degrees.

"Welcome to Idaho, sweet baby," we had said, as she slept beneath fuzzy snowsuits and baby blankets. Now, two weeks later, I sat in the familiar handicap spot outside my school campus. My younger sister, Anna, sat next to me in the passenger seat.

"Okay," she said. "What should I do to help? Should I grab the baby?"

"Actually, no." I smiled, handing her my phone. "I want you to film. I want people to know it's possible to do something like this by yourself."

She nodded, stepping back a few feet to get the full picture—disabled mom in academic robe, easing out of the driver's seat, shambling down the side of the car toward its back door. I was so flustered I realized halfway there I had left the engine running. I turned, retraced my path, and red-faced, grabbed the key. I had rehearsed this moment in my mind throughout my whole pregnancy—now to see if it would work.

Opening the back door, I pulled out my wheelchair, unfolded it, and settled into place. From the other side of the car, Hadassah's wails broke through the winter air, insistent and needy. I fumbled with the straps of my baby carrier and readied it around my shoulders. I still struggled to wear it right. Hadassah still struggled with being worn. Neither of us was an expert at anything baby-related at this point.

I rolled around to her side, opened the door, and started working on the car seat. We had chosen it carefully—a rotating base that allowed me, from my wheelchair, to swivel it outward, unbuckle her, and lift her to my chest. An ambulatory parent may have found such a seat impractical, as it couldn't be lifted out like a carrier—but that didn't matter for me. I couldn't carry a car seat while pushing a wheelchair anyway. With this setup, we didn't even need a stroller.

Hadassah's wails rose to a crescendo as I lifted her out, maneuvering her into the wraps of my baby carrier with fumbling hands. I reached for my schoolbag—now stuffed with diapers, wipes, and a nursing apron on top of my textbooks—slung it over my wheelchair handles, and rolled forward. The baby wrap left my hands free to maneuver my chair. In case you don't know and need to—babywearing is a wheelchair user's best parenting hack.

Two terms stood between me and graduation. And now, I would finish strong—with a baby strapped to my chest.

My professors broke open doors often locked to mothers like me. They considered my needs and limitations with care, then allowed me to bring my newborn to class—even when it meant missing two-thirds of the lecture to soothe her cries. They bent deadlines, let me take finals remotely—unheard-of at my rigorous private school—and extended grace where chaos threatened to take over. Without them, I never would have made it through.

For anyone who believes "the system" crushes the possibility of change, consider this: The system didn't get this disabled mama across the stage. Rather, a handful of professors chose compassion over convention, thought creatively through each obstacle, and came to meet me when elevators could not. Nervous, apologetic, and exhausted, I often sat just outside the classroom door, rocking Hadassah in my wheelchair, offering her a bottle, pleading with her to sleep, trying to calm those newborn wails. Believe me, a cheerful smile and understanding nod go a long way.

My mornings were mayhem: taking my medication, eating breakfast, changing diapers, trying to push my shaky legs into old shoes and Hadassah's wiggling ones into a cute onesie. She often curled up and napped on my chest while I typed my papers and thesis one-handed, praying I could find the words that dodged my sleep-deprived brain.

When graduation day arrived, it was still full of chaos and blatantly *unacademic* activities. I pumped breast milk right before I zipped up my graduation gown, curled my hair while bouncing the baby in the swing with my foot, and applied my lipstick right before I grabbed Jeeves—my first cane—who had gotten me through school and that whole first year of disability and deployment.

Before the graduates' names were called, the rewards for outstanding students were announced. Four names. One of them was mine. I rolled to the front of the room in my wheelchair and sat there, feeling as if I was sitting inside someone else's success story, while my theology professor read the anonymous testimony of other professors and faculty.

> Sydney is, of course, excellent academically, but her dedication and perseverance in the face of health issues are inspiring. Being a new mom on top of that makes her dedication that much more impressive, and one of the highlights of the year was to see Sydney's baby daughter, Hadassah, sitting in her mom's lap during recitation, her little face peeking over the table.

Oh yes—my greatest achievement with a hair bow. My little Dassie, who surely deserves college credit for the number of lectures she sat through. She heard my senior thesis. Listened to lessons on Keynes, Homer, and Nietzsche. She attended my finals—curled in my lap while I wrote—wide-eyed and drooling onto Kant and math questions. I wonder if her big baby eyes ever scored me a more merciful grade when the sleep deprivation and brain fog caught up to me.

> Sydney takes all her sufferings and turns them into gold . . .

These trembling legs and this wheeled frame I was so afraid others might see, God turned into gold *in their eyes too*. God takes what we fear will mark us as weak and makes it a testimony of His greatness.

> Sydney is an inspiration to others through the lovely combination of excellence and grace, which shine through in all that she does.

> More than any other student I can remember, Sydney has modeled Christian cheer and perseverance in the face of trial.

People are watching you. They see your smiles, your poise, your limp, your laughter. They see your confidence even as you're spasming and jerking or rolling. They see your humor. They see God in your suffering. Your existence testifies—your pain, your joy, your hope. People see God not only in your thriving—but even more so, in how you struggle with faith.

And then, the only professor I was able to guess—Dr. Schlect, the one whose class literally had me scaling mountains, whose total belief and investment in me led me to get my wheelchair in the first place.

> I asked the students how Thucydides might feel with the situation in Ukraine. Where most other students sized up the international balance of power, Sydney went further by proposing specific strategies, troop deployments, allocations of material, and field tactics. That day I learned a new postulate of political realism: Hell hath no fury like a married woman, whose husband is stationed overseas, in a final exam.

He wasn't wrong; that final came right after Colton's deployment extended. So I had a *very* personal bias against Putin.

> I wonder if the reason why Sydney took to her cane and then to her wheelchair was an effort to make things more fair for the rest of us. Sydney's infirmities only make her better, and she has a mysterious way of making everyone around her better as well.

When they called my name, I pushed myself out of my wheelchair to walk across the stage, cane in hand. Colton stood beside me as my support, physically representing on this stage what he had been to me behind the scenes all these years. I leaned into him as we stepped forward. My legs weren't steady, but he was. And for once, we weren't rushing. We weren't surviving. We were arriving somewhere. Somewhere good.

I crossed that stage as a mother. A graduate. A woman who had been carried—not just by her husband or a wheelchair or professors or students, but by God Himself. Carried through doubt, exhaustion, and pain. Carried when I couldn't see how this could end in anything but collapse and failure.

The words from my professors meant more to me than a *summa cum laude* designation. The weight of their witness, the affection in their words, wrapped around me like armor. The battle, the deployment, the seizures, the exhaustion, the baby at home—they made this moment more than a graduation. I had gained far more than a college degree.

Thank God for all the people who don't flinch at the mess, or the wheelchair, or the wailing baby.

Thank God that *He* doesn't. He never does.

And then, Colton and I stepped off the stage. Into whatever would come next.

SEVENTEEN

together

I have to learn how to talk in front of my one-year-old. I refuse to be embarrassed by a lesson she is learning too.

A: a-a-a.

B: ba-ba-ba.

Sound out the words. Letter by letter.

One sound at a time.

It's okay if your mouth gets the sounds wrong. It's okay to stumble through our stories. It's all part of learning how to speak, how to read, how to tell a good one.

Mama will show you. These are good things to learn.

Sometimes I want to give up. Sometimes the process is excruciating. But if I start to cry, stumbling and slurring my sounds over *Winnie-the-Pooh*, snap the book shut, and say, "I'm done. This is too hard. I give up on this reading thing," she will learn *that* lesson instead. When it's hard to read and she struggles one day with her own words, she will have learned that the process isn't worth it; reading and speaking aren't worth the pain they take to learn.

And when that time comes, how will I ask her to keep *Winnie-the-Pooh* open, to embrace all that words can do for her in life, to say, "Today is *Winnie-the-Pooh*, but one day, it will be the whole story"? How can I tell her it's worth it for her to learn if it's not worth it for me to *re*learn? So many lessons—lessons bigger than speaking, than reading, than walking. Lessons about what is important in this world, how good gifts are heavy sometimes, how stumbling and falling are part of the process and not part of the failure, and how good it is to fight for these basic things, because these are the fundamentals to everything else.

"In the beginning was the Word, and the Word was with God, and the Word was God" (John 1:1). Words matter—as a thing more fundamental than matter. Here, Hadassah: God gave us words. I know they are hard to say sometimes. Mama struggles too. But we will fight for this together, because the reward is worth fighting for.

So are your legs.

So is your smile.

So is getting out of bed in the morning.

So is this life.

Our brokenness is not beautiful or wonderful because it feels good. It is beautiful and wonderful because, one day, it will be redeemed. And redemption is so powerful, it works backward through time. Very few things in this world can do that, but redemption does. Knowing that one day, *this* body, and *this* brokenness, and *this* pain, and *this* struggle will all be redeemed *is* the glory that works back through time and renews us in each present moment. Without the future glory, all the present pain is meaningless. With the future glory, all the present pain is glorified.

Through wheelchairs and walking, falls and fruitfulness, cups of tea and college boys lifting wheelchair litters over mountain battlefields, through kind professors and crying newborns, through the bite of hospital dismissals and the brilliance of cane-naming friends—God makes fearful things wonderful, and in this world, He makes them so side by side.

This is what we know because we are in Christ: Broken things don't stay broken. The final glory we look forward to with slow, shallow, bated breath works backward until, even now—like sunlight spilling through a cracked door into a dusty room—it touches every particle of brokenness and makes it dance and glimmer with meaning.

That glory works backward to give *this* moment purpose. *That* beauty makes your wobbly legs worth it. *That* wonder makes your stumbling words holy. *That* promise makes this life—one filled with concentrated, body-destroying pain—the vessel of concentrated, soul-exalting glory.

So we turn the page.

We speak the next word.

We take the next step.

Because the One who began a good work in us will carry it on to completion (Philippians 1:6). Not despite the brokenness—but because of it. Our brokenness is fearful and wonderful because He is using it to make all things whole.

A Strong King

Hadassah is learning about strength from me—because she is seeing my weakness. She is learning about walking because she sees me fall. About fighting because she sees me rest. About living because she sees a daily kind of dying. I don't try to teach her—"You can do anything! You are strong, you are brave, you are beautiful all on your own! See how *Mama* does all these things? That is because Mama won't let anything stop her!"

No. Oh, no, my sweet girl. May you never bear the burden of that lie.

Mama is weak, but Jesus is strong. Mama can't do anything on her own—but she has tried. Oh, she has tried many times. And do you know what she has found? She has to rely on Jesus. Jesus is doing it all. He is holding Mama up. He is strengthening her legs to walk, and He strengthens her heart when it crumbles. Mama is very weak, very afraid, very broken sometimes, but Jesus is so good and so mighty, He makes Mama strong, and brave, and beautiful because *He* is. See how *Jesus* does all these things? That is because nothing can stop Him!

And when you are weak, my sweet daughter, when your heart feels broken, or your body, or your soul, remember it is not your strength; the strength is Jesus'. Go to Him with your weakness, your fear, your brokenness. Your dependence on Him is the sweetest lesson you can learn. This whole life is about learning dependence and learning it well. Sometimes Jesus will teach you in ways that hurt, but in the end, that hurt will resound with glory.

You are going to run a race your whole life—the same race Mama is running, even from her wheelchair, even from her bed. You will run a race against unbelief. You can do that when you are full of human energy, and you can do that when you are flat on your back at the end of your strength. When you finish this race—when you cross the finish line—you will most likely be flat on your back. You won't have anything left to give, and that is the best place to be, because it means you are ready to receive everything Jesus has to offer. If the race is won in your bed, take heart: Jesus is the Lord of broken bedsides.

When I was a kid, my dad taught us the questions and answers of the Children's Shorter Catechism. We memorized everything up through question and answer 136. There were some tough ones in there; I was proud when I could recite the lengthy second and fourth commandments word for word. The Lord's Prayer had many petitions. The theology around the sacraments was deep. But the hardest questions for me to answer were questions 68 and 71.

They weren't long; they were just hard for me to say out loud. It *hurt* to answer them. As an active, outdoorsy, and energetic tomboy, I prided myself on my physical strength and stamina. I spent hours flipping hay bales with my dad and grandpa. I processed animals, trained horses, hiked and hunted for miles in the wilderness. I finished a 5K feeling as giddy and refreshed as when I started. I learned martial arts from my dad and single-handedly took down every boy at our church when they got snarky—including those bigger, stronger, and older than me. I even prided myself at having known and memorized the *most* catechism questions and answers, so when we got to the infamous 60s, Dad would look up from his book, right at me, and smile.

"Sydney," he would say, not breaking eye contact, "how is Christ a king?"

"Because He rules over us and defends us."

"And Sydney . . ." He would pause, smiling deeper, both love and challenge in his eyes. "*Why* do you need Christ as a king?"

Then I would meet his gaze and say through clenched teeth: "Because I am *weak* and *helpless*."[1]

The spiritual truth was a harrowing reality, shoved beneath years of physical strength. Weak and helpless—but, oh, watch me run, watch me climb, watch me flip hay bales. Weak and helpless to *God*, maybe—but independent, strong, brave, fast, a fighter all on my own. Weak and helpless in *Christ*, maybe, but not by any human standard of strength—*surely* not by my standard. I could admit the spiritual reality through gritted teeth, but I'd rather grit my teeth as I reined in a flighty horse or pounded open the ice on a frozen water trough. The hardest teeth-gritting absolutes were the words that admitted my weakness.

I lost it all. Oh, I lost it all. I lost the strength to run—and the strength to walk. To stand on my own two feet. I lost the strength to climb—unless the often insurmountable distance between a floor and a wheelchair transfer can count. I lost the strength to train, to glory, to exult in myself. Still the same person inside—the same independent go-getter, do-it-all and do-it-all-well person, trapped in a body that can only do it barely and badly. Suffocated in my own weakness—for stifled beneath layers of pain is a heart that still aches to do something.

I had always been able to stuff down the reality of my own weakness—a reality that felt purely spiritual, ethereal, abstract. Now my weakness confronts me every day, closer than skin and bone. It is the realest thing about my physical body. The only constant. The imprisonment of everything else. I am weak, I am weak, I am weak. But, oh! I have a King.

"How is Christ my King?" I whisper in bed, gasping out the words, racked by convulsions.

Because He rules over me and defends me.

Why do I need Christ as a King?

And here is the balm—the sweet balm, the admission that is true, *true* more than anything, true and therefore good, sacred, redeemable: *Because I am weak and helpless.*

I put one Scripture reference on my Instagram profile: 2 Corinthians 12:9—"He said to me, 'My grace is sufficient for you, for my power is made perfect in weakness.' Therefore I will boast all the more gladly about my weaknesses, so that Christ's power may rest on me" (NIV).

Here is my banner. Here is my boast: "I am weak and I am *glad*, for Christ's power rests upon me. His power is made perfect in my weakness."

I engraved this verse onto two of my canes—the perfect physical illustration of everything I have lost and gained. "Here is my cane—my weakness. Emblazoned upon it is the promise—God's strength."

One day my canes—my beautiful canes, which I have grown to love in their own right—will be splintered and broken and pounded into a cross of glory. One day my wheelchair—my life-changing wheelchair—will be melted down into a crucible of redemption. I look forward to the day when I'll stand above my life-saving devices, my physical supports through a long and weary road, and see them turned to matchwood, molten metal, and paint.

I can't wait to step over the pile of rubble and pain, look into the eyes of Jesus, and hear Him bless me—not in spite of my weakness but because of it. I can't wait for Jesus to find strength in me—not my strength but His—the only strength, the best strength, forged through bedridden days and years of limping, forged through my weakest, strength-lacking moments, redeemed in a fire that melted my body like wax.

Jesus rates strength differently than we do. He uses His own standard. He holds strength up against Himself. Let Him only find His strength in us, when He holds us up in glory.

EIGHTEEN

wings

I sat in bed, my journal open before me on the sheets. Long day. *Long* day. Hadassah had been fussy and clingy. I was exhausted but felt as though *nothing* had gotten done. When Colton came home, I expected to feel better, but every little thing annoyed me.

"What is wrong with everyone?" I wanted to scream. I tried to redirect my irritation into a more *spiritual* direction. I had gotten into the habit of writing my prayers, so I picked up my pen and began writing a long prayer that I intended to be a confession of my exasperation and irritability throughout the day.

Hadassah did this, and I snapped at her. Colton said this, and it bothered me so much. My confession was derailing—it was spiraling into an unholy rant session before the Lord.

Lord, I don't understand why I feel this way. I haven't felt this irritated and mad at the world since—

Oh my gosh, I'm pregnant!

Sure enough, the next morning, I stared at two pink lines in the bathroom while Hadassah cooed and played in the next room. She had turned one *two days before*. This was a bit fast, wasn't it? I wasn't ready to be pregnant with a toddler. I wasn't ready to be pregnant, *period*. And then two under two? Good grief. How was I going to make it? This was insanity. I only had one lap.

If I'm holding baby number two on my wheelchair, then where is Hadassah supposed to go? What if they run in opposite directions? What if I'm having a seizure and they both start crying? What if I'm exhausted, and one is tired and one is hungry, and I'm in so much pain I can barely function?

I was getting into a groove with Hadassah. I had just gotten a rhythm. It was working. But the rhythm wouldn't work with two. All the plans, the routines, the strategies . . . I had to start from scratch?

Healthy parents struggle with this short age gap. Gosh, the first trimester had *floored* me last time—and that was when I could rest whenever I wanted. Now I had a toddler to take care of. For hours of the day, resting was not an option. And midnight feedings *again*? Starting over. Starting from scratch. Right when things were starting to get easier. I had reached my new post-baby weight. I had *just* bought new jeans!

Had I not been in a state of complete shock and resignation, I might have sprung the news on Colton differently. Instead, he walked in from a 6:00 a.m. work meeting, and I picked Hadassah up off the floor.

"Look how big she's getting. Can you believe she's a big sister now?"

Colton's jaw dropped.

I am still being sanctified.

Pregnancy Symptom: Doubt

Depression haunted me for twelve weeks. Guilt dogged depression's heels. *How am I depressed? I love this baby, don't I?* During my pregnancy with Hadassah, I thought of her constantly. Now I'm so busy, sometimes I forget I'm pregnant. I feel sick and miserable and so ... exhausted. This is already so hard, and it's only going to get harder, isn't it? I know what pregnancy with Hadassah was like—one nine-month-long flare. I'm not ready for nine months of flare with a toddler. How will I even get through the day? But then, this is a real baby, after all. Why don't I feel more excitement? More love? More connection?

"What is wrong with me?" I would ask Colton when doubt weighed heavily. "Am I a horrible person? Am I a horrible mother?"

"No, you're a tired mother," Colton would say. "Let me take Hadassah for a little bit."

Three hours later, I would come out of the room to blocks and stuffed animals scattered across the floor, Hadassah on Colton's lap while he entertained her with anything and everything from Dr. Seuss to live streamed Senate sessions off of YouTube.

"She did pretty good," Colton would say, giving me the rundown. "She had two meltdowns—one when her giraffe fell on the floor, and then one when I got up to use the bathroom. She had one smelly diaper and finished her bottle of milk. She said 'mama' once—but 'dada' like nineteen times. I think she missed you—and she's tired. Also, she really liked the video I showed her of the gorilla. We read *Hop on Pop* twice and then needed a break, so we read the Constitution for fun." (Colton meant that in all sincerity. By the time she was three weeks old, Hadassah had "read" the Constitution and the Declaration of Independence multiple times, had the Bill of Rights clearly explained to her, and of course, had heard the book of Esther—her namesake.)

We didn't tell anyone about the second baby for the first three months. I knew people would be surprised, doubting my ability to take this on, wondering what on earth we were thinking. I wasn't ready to face their concerns and questions when I was wondering the exact same thing.

"Are you ready for kid number two?"

"No. No, I'm not. But what am I going to do? Send it back?"

I needed time. Time to carry this alone, to process, to fall in love with this idea before I shared it with others. The time alone brought quiet, which I needed, but it was also terribly isolating. By the end of the twelve weeks, I wasn't sure if staying quiet was the right call after all, but I kept reminding myself I wasn't strong enough yet to hear my own doubts spoken out loud.

As we told people who reacted well—first our two families—my confidence grew. It felt more real now, that this was a person, a real person whom I was carrying, holding, loving. I wasn't just sick and miserable; I was sick and miserable *for a reason*. This pregnancy would end in another little baby, whom I would love as I loved Hadassah. I entered the second trimester, somehow still losing weight. My symptoms were bad, flaring, terrible, and I was exhausted all the time—but it felt more real. This baby. This new life. All of this pain for a reason. A wonderful, beautiful, glorious reason—the tiny little person growing inside me.

I would figure it out. Wheelchair logistics hadn't made much sense before I held Hadassah in my arms, but they fell into place. I learned on the job—as all parents do. I just had to learn different things. The routines, the rhythms, the strategies would come—not too soon, not before their time, but not too late either. I could trust the Lord in that.

I would see Hadassah playing and think, *Oh, I can do two. No problem. I love the idea of two!*

But when she whined and hung on my legs while I was trying to cook with a hot pan from my wheelchair, despair filled my heart. *Oh, no—two! How will I do two? This is insane! This is impossible!*

Thankfully, God is not on an emotional roller coaster. He doesn't fluctuate with a toddler's nap schedule. And He certainly doesn't second-guess His perfect plans.

My belly may have been rising and swelling with pregnancy and anxiety—but that little baby continued to be fearfully and wonderfully formed in my womb.

163

Colton had to leave for a fifteen-day military training near the end of the first trimester, which meant his *Hop on Pop* and Constitutional readings were on pause for a while. It was a long two weeks, made two days longer than necessary due to a mix-up in military orders. I'm not sure who felt it more—me or Hadassah. We had just bought a house twenty minutes away in the small town of Troy, Idaho—a farmhouse on seven thousand square feet, where we had plans for keeping chickens, a garden, and a rooster—if Colton could convince the city to change the rooster code for us.

While he was gone, I had more big plans for establishing a new cleaning routine, packing up boxes, and getting everything ready for the upcoming move. My plans fell by the wayside as reality struck: Pregnancy with a toddler—a toddler who was afraid of the sound of packing tape, no less—was not conducive to mustering the energy a move demanded. Then we both got hit with the stomach flu.

Vomiting into the kitchen trash can and changing seven explosive diarrhea diapers a day would have tipped my strength over the line, except for one, absolute toddler miracle: Hadassah's sleep changed.

Suddenly, my little six a.m. alarm clock slept in till eight, then nine, then ten. Three days in a row. Three hours later, I would put her to sleep, and she would sleep another four or five hours. Then fall back asleep again with no problem that night. I knew she was sick and probably needed the extra rest, so I thanked God for the timing of this present disaster and took the extra hours of rest with fear and trembling. When her symptoms disappeared, however, and her new sleep schedule continued, I started to get a little worried. The extra hours were wonderful—they were keeping my body going—but was everything okay? Fourteen hours a night? Five hours a day? My fourteen-month-old was sleeping a solid eighteen hours out of twenty-four. I took her to see her pediatrician.

"My guess is she's still fighting something," he said after he examined her. "Track her wake windows and her diaper changes. Give her another week. The stomach virus going around is nasty and lingers long. I saw another girl her age who had it for almost three weeks!"

"But all her other symptoms are gone," I said. "It's just *sleeping*."

"Give her time," he said. "If you don't see any change next week, bring her back and we can test if she still has the virus."

I did. I gave her time. I felt bad for my sweet little baby—except she seemed to be doing *great*. She had no other symptoms. She was happy, energetic, active, eating again. She just slept a ton. For no apparent reason.

Lord, please bless Hadassah with a good, long nap, I had prayed that first morning, exhausted, giving her a kiss as I tucked her in. *Because both of us really need to rest.*

I sang and prayed with her and then crawled straight to my own bed, pulled up the covers, and slept as long as she let me. When she woke up for her next wake window, I did what I could—played, rested, cleaned. Then nap time again. Same prayer. *Lord, we both need to rest.*

Every nap time I prayed this prayer. And now, here she was, for no apparent reason, *sleeping* all hours of the day and night. I was getting up *before* her, before her naps ended, feeling okay, feeling more energized. It was always just enough to get me through the next wake window. And then we would both sleep and sleep and *sleep*. Wake up. Repeat. Day after day. No changes.

"Where is Hadassah? I want to talk to her!" Colton said on FaceTime.

"She's still sleeping."

"She's *always* sleeping! I wanna see my Squish!"

"I know," I said, in true wonder. "I know, but it's also—helping *a lot*."

One night, the extra sleep wasn't enough. I lay in bed and felt the seizure coming on—and I knew it would be a bad one. My coherence was slipping. I started to lose touch with where I was and what was real. Darkness clouded my vision. I couldn't move. Physical feelings of fear rose up in my body as it fought for control, fought to remain on the surface of consciousness, fought against the pain. Losing coherence is always terrifying, but especially so when you are alone.

I knew surrender was inevitable. As I sank into the darkness, lies would be whispering in my ears. Nightmarish dreams and hallucinations played across my mind and body, as my brain tried to make sense of the pain with the slipping rubric of conscious thought and reality. I had little to no control of the fear I experienced or the images I saw. They were sheer, physical, involuntary responses to pain and cognitive compromise.

But I also knew what was coming. I knew I was going under—but the *going*—that was a different story. *Going under*—as I felt mental capacity fading, my body slipping out of my control, the convulsions and confusion setting their net around me—I could plead out loud to God. I did then, tears streaming down my face, my breath coming in raspy wheezes through the convulsions.

"God, I'm losing it again. I'm getting scared. I'm so scared. I know I'm going to get worse until my seizure comes. God, I won't be able to hold on to You when it comes for me. Please hold on to me. Go with me into the darkness. Please hold me, God. Please hold me!"

My words slurred. I was awake, but I could speak no longer. Images flashed. The nightmares.

Think of something good. Think of someone you love. No—no, please! Not like that! No—stop! I was sobbing. I was losing control. *God, please hold me, God, please hold me!*

The images shifted, morphing with my prayer. I saw God in judgment, God angry, God bringing a dark hand over my face. I screamed. *God, I know that's not You. Please help me to know You. Help me to know You right now.*

I couldn't pray anymore. It was too terrifying. I knew the images weren't real, but praying in this moment was making them worse. I knew my prayer from earlier would carry me through. I knew God would hold me, even when I couldn't pray.

One. O-N-E.

Two. T-W-O.

I counted in my head. Sometimes out loud. Stuttering. Slurring. Sobbing.

Twenty-three. T-W-E-N-T . . . T-T . . . Y.

Count. Count. Spell. Spell. Don't stop. Don't think. Stutter your way through the madness until it's over.

Fifty-four. F-F-F . . . no, stop, please! F-F-F-I . . . yes, that's it. I-F . . . f again. Wait—how many fs are in fifty-four? So many fs—too many fs, isn't it? T-Y-YYYYY . . . shut up. Please. F-F-F . . . I think. F . . . right? F . . . again?

Don't stop. Don't stop. Don't let the fact that it doesn't make sense scare you. None of it will make sense. Fifty-four is an easy number. It's basic. But it has a lot of fs, and that's not your fault. Keep going. Keep breathing.

F-F-F.

I counted and spelled my way up to 163. Then the letters slurred and slowed, and my breath became more shallow. I tried to finish the letter but couldn't, and I fell into the darkness.

I couldn't pray inside there. I couldn't sing. I couldn't think clearly. I couldn't even count. A long, terrifying silence swallowed my mind. Images without words, without sound. Terror. Pain. Let me out. Let me out. Please.

I had two more seizures before I was coherent again.

God no longer held terror for me. He knew me. He was there.

"God, thank You for holding me." My cheeks were still wet with tears. "Thank You for being real, and true, and good even when I can't understand what is happening. Thank You for letting me know, even in that confusion, that what I saw wasn't You. Thank You for answering my prayer."

I turned on a John Piper sermon and pulled the blankets close. I stared at the ceiling, at the shadows over my bed. I listened to the pastor's voice, and I thought about God, holding me in the darkness.

The day after Colton got home, Hadassah's sleep pattern returned to normal.

Strength to Walk

When I prayed that God would hold me fast, He was already doing it. Maybe you don't have seizures, but you, too, can feel when you are entering a darkness you can't control: a spiral of grief, a hard anniversary, a dangerous surgery, a particularly difficult day. And you may cry to God to enter that darkness and pain with you. The *going under* may be terrifying, but it may also sink you into the Rock of Ages.

You are not sinning when dark thoughts assault you. You are not sinning by grieving, by sobbing, by wanting things to be different. It is what you *do* with these thoughts, these desires, this grief, that determines whether it is sin or glory.

John Milton—best known as the author of the greatest poem in the English language, *Paradise Lost*—became blind. In the middle of his life's calling, he lost his sight. He felt the loss in himself, and he felt the loss of what he could give for the sake of the kingdom. Through his daughter, he wrote a sonnet about his own devastating blindness.

> When I consider how my light is spent,
> Ere half my days, in this dark world and wide,
> And that one Talent which is death to hide
> Lodged with me useless, though my Soul more bent
> To serve therewith my Maker . . .[1]

O Lord, that's all I wanted with my strength—I just wanted to serve You! I could be a better mother without this disease. I could do more for Hadassah. I could play longer hours. I'm sure I could support her better, and work harder, and teach her more. Yet I am a mother debilitated, a wife debilitated, a Christian debilitated. And how will I now . . .

> . . . present
> My true account, lest he returning chide;
> "Doth God exact day-labour, light denied?"[2]

God does not demand the task for which He does not provide the strength.

> But patience, to prevent
> That murmur, soon replies, "God doth not need
> Either man's work or his own gifts; who best
> Bear his mild yoke, they serve him best.[3]

O Lord, You don't need my work. I need Your work. You don't need my brokenness. I need Your wholeness. You don't need my empty offerings of strength. I need Your abundance. God doesn't need my own version of success, for . . .

> . . . His state
> Is Kingly. Thousands at his bidding speed
> And post o'er Land and Ocean without rest:
> They also serve who only stand and wait.[4]

They also serve who only stand and wait. I serve God when I stand and wait.

Hadassah watches the walking sessions now. When the daytime fussiness and sleep deprivation and midnight check-ins after sudden wails get to be too much, and my seizures bring back the incoherence, and the paralysis, and the loss of feeling, I roll over and touch Colton's arm and say, "Help," and I lie in bed with Hadassah on one side and Colton on the other.

Before Hadassah was born, I was scared thinking about when this would happen in front of her. Would it be scary for her? How much would she understand? It doesn't scare me anymore. I know what I will tell her:

> Have you not known?
> Have you not heard?
> The everlasting God, the LORD,
> The Creator of the ends of the earth.
> Neither faints nor is weary.
> His understanding is unsearchable.
> He gives power to the weak,
> And to those who have no might He increases strength.
> Even the youths shall faint and be weary,
> And the young men shall utterly fall,
> But those who wait on the LORD
> Shall renew their strength;
> They shall mount up with wings like eagles,
> They shall run and not be weary,
> They shall walk and not faint. (Isaiah 40:28–31)

It used to confuse me that the verse goes from running to walking. Isn't running the more impressive thing? Shouldn't the order of language build—we walk, we run, we mount up with wings? Why end with the lesser promise? Why end with saying we will know how to walk?

I understand now. It is not the lesser promise. Mounting up with wings is glorious; running is fleet and thus is easy. Walking is the hard thing. To walk and not be faint—that's what we must do our whole life through. That is the thing that most tempts us to faint, that most exhausts us. "Lord, give me strength to run!" is the easy prayer—the exciting prayer—the prayer with clear, glorious answers—the faith-building ones that border on miraculous.

"Lord, give me strength to walk." How often do we pray this prayer? In the day-to-day, the moment to moment, not up on mountains but wading through sagebrush, thinking we are strong enough to keep moving without clinging to Him, not realizing it is His strength—and only His strength—that upholds us for the walking. Faithful. New every morning.

"Mommy's legs don't work well," I tell Hadassah. Her mouth opens in a toothy smile, and she giggles blushingly. "No, they don't," I say, laughing with her. "One day soon you will walk and run even though Mommy can't very well." I pick her up and set her on my lap, unlocking the brakes on my wheelchair. We roll through the house, her fuzzy head pressed up against my chest, my hand on her stomach, the other on the wheel rims.

"Should we go fast?" I ask her. She loves the ride. Even when she's fussy and won't let anyone sit down with her, I can sit with her on the wheelchair and take us in big circles around the house. She soothes, nestled against my stomach, her tiny fingers in her mouth or around my fingers. She developed an amazing center of balance early on, and now I can turn, spin, and wheelie without her so much as teetering or breaking her relaxed, stoic expression.

Mount up with wings. What will it be like when she can walk and run? When she's no longer content to sit on my lap? Will I be able to keep up with her from my chair? Well—I'll have to. I don't have a choice. What a glorious thing to have such decisions made for me.

God often forces me to accept gifts outside my comfort zone. Those are the best kind—the ones I need Him to carry.

Run and not be weary. Yes, you will run one day, Hadassah. But the most important race is the one we run together, before God, before the cross, before a cloud of witnesses.

Walk and not be faint. I know so well what it is to walk and be faint, but my weakness is my glory, for in my weakness is His strength. His mercies are new every morning. Great is His faithfulness.

"Yes, sweet girl," I whisper, kissing the top of her round fuzzy head against my chest. I open the front door, and sunlight streams through the glass, illuminating the room, the books, the houseplants along the fireplace mantel, the soft skin of the toddler on my lap.

"I love being your mama."

And I know, as I turn the page in this love story, that having a daughter is teaching me to be one.

First Page

Hadassah has a little rocking giraffe that she likes to ride on now. Our second daughter is due in two months, and the rocker is the perfect third-trimester toy for us. Dassie drags it over to me while I sit on the couch. I help her on, lean back, and close my eyes, then rock her with my toes—back and forth, back and forth, back and forth.

The eyes-closed session seldom lasts long. Hadassah doesn't want to just *ride* the giraffe. She wants to know what everything on the giraffe is *called*—over and over. As she points to each part in front of her, I start giving her the names I've told her a hundred times: "Yes, yes, Dassie. Horns. Ears. Handles. Eyes. Spot." Once she runs out of giraffe, she starts pointing to the parts of *me* she can reach—usually: "Knee. Yes, Dassie. Other knee."

After that, the process begins all over again, round and round the front half of the giraffe she goes. She can't see the second half, behind her, so that goes unnamed for the moment. I'm pretty sure she knows all the words now; she just wants to hear *me* say them. Horns will stay horns, you know, but in toddler land, that's magical stuff.

Sometimes my prayers to God are like that. I know certain promises—ones I can see, remember, ones so familiar to me I can say them in baby talk and half-murmured sentences: "The LORD is my shepherd; I shall not want . . . Trust in the LORD with all your heart, and lean not on your own understanding . . . He shall be like a tree, planted by rivers of water . . . Fear not, for I am with you; be not dismayed, for I am your God . . . And the peace of God, which transcends all understanding, will guard your hearts your and minds . . . For God so loved the world He gave His only begotten Son . . ."[5]

Sometimes I come boldly, knowing that because of Christ, I can approach God's throne of grace without fear, that He will hear me, for He has given His Son. How much more shall He not also give me all things (Romans 8:32)? Other times, I come trembling. Like David praying before God, sometimes my prayers are a whispered: "You, O LORD of hosts, God of Israel, have revealed this to Your servant . . . Therefore Your servant has found it in his heart to pray this prayer to You" (2 Samuel 7:27).

O Lord, You have already promised this. That's how I got the gall to ask.

God rejoices in prayers like that. As you go into the rest of your life, the rest of your suffering, the rest of your glory—remind God of His promises to you. Like a toddler on a rocking giraffe, name what you see, name what you know, and name it over and over again.

Because this is not your full story. This is the cover. This is the title page. You haven't even begun chapter one yet. Chapter one is beautiful. It is so beautiful that one day, when you see it, you will look back at the cover and say, "I see now. I see now why the cover looks this way. I see now why this is the title page: *Fearfully and Wonderfully Broken*."

Now we see the broken.

Soon we will see the wonderful.

Just like how one day, Hadassah will discover there's a whole lot of giraffe behind her—including the part that, this whole time, has been holding her up.

a prayer for when you're still fighting for faith

What follows is not a conclusion because, well, there isn't one. Not yet. Not for me and not for you. Our story is still going, and we don't know what the Author will write for us, tonight, or tomorrow, or years from now.

Sometimes sorrows and prayers come out in poem fragments for me, which I think is fitting being that fragments are, at times, all we can hold.

Following is just such a "fragment" that came to mind in a dark night of fighting after a long and weary day. I hope we can hold it together and offer it to God. I hope to sit beside you in the darkness and point you to the light.

Like Jacob, we have been touched by the Son of God. In our brokenness is blessing. In our pain is promise. In our wrestling is redemption. Hold onto God with me and wait:

The day is dark,
and my soul,
cracked—

a prayer for when you're still fighting for faith

grief-devoured,
sorrow-bitten,
aches in the gloaming of the hour
like weary joints
before the rain,
an old temple
in a young storm.

My sorrow
lies before me,
as old as I am,
with me every day
of every year,
of every moment.

And sometimes it is hard
to remember
that though my sorrows
are years and years,
God's grace
lies eternal—
God's grace as old
as God.

When I am locked outside the city
with no pillow for
my weary head,
and I hear the gates lock shut,
and I think:

There is no safe place,
no home for me,

no consolation
in the desolation
of this life—

I feel the grip
of the Son of God,
and I grab His heel
and say,

“I will not let You go
until You bless me.”

—*Sydney Anne Bennett,*
during a night of fighting, 2017

until we rise

So many hands have carried me (some literally!). So many hearts have reminded me of God's faithfulness along the way.

Colton, the love of my life—thank you for everything. For asking for my email address that first day like good homeschoolers should, for encouraging me, comforting me, and pointing me to the Lord through our years of friendship, dating, and engagement. For loving me as no one else could through the eleven of the first fourteen months of our marriage spent oceans apart, for making me laugh at your weird jokes, for holding me through discouragement and seizures, and for walking with me through the same symptoms and struggles again and again. Thank you for making me feel beautiful in hospital gowns—and right now, eight months pregnant. I love you.

Hadassah, thank you for making me a mama when I didn't know I could be one. For giggling at my limps, tremors, and weird symptoms so I can see the humor in them and giggle too. For loving my wheelchair, for dragging me outside on my bad-symptom days, forcing me to slow down, and in short, making me do things that make me feel better that I don't want to do. For being my absolute JOY, beautiful girl. I love you. I'm so blessed to be your mama.

Felicity, you're not born yet, but I can't wait to meet you soon, my beautiful girl. Love overwhelms me when I remember that at the end of these nine months, I get to hold you. See you soon, sweet daughter.

My parents, who have loved me beautifully, wonderfully, and unconditionally all my life. For laying and exemplifying a foundation of faith that could stand the fiery trials ahead. For the countless prayers, ripe with the heartfulness only a parent can feel. For the thousands of big and small and immensely practical blessings—flights back and forth to help me move, driving to and from Idaho countless times during Colton's deployment and after, meals, flowers, gifts, and words of encouragement sent from afar, phone calls and unwavering devotion, and even an air conditioner to get me through these last miserable months of summer pregnancy. As a parent now, I hold more love and admiration for you than ever before. As a parent now, I have even fewer words to express them. I love you.

My siblings:

Maya, for phone calls, for Potato Peel Society–inspired letters during Colton's deployment, and for staying one step ahead in motherhood so I can follow your wisdom. And for talking books and writing with me like we did when we were little.

Audrey, for your practical advice and encouragement, for never forgetting to ask about this manuscript even while basking on beaches in Hawaii, and for finding such creative solutions so I could be in your wedding. I love seeing the unfolding of the life God has for you.

Anna, for being someone I can tell anything to—I know you'll always be on my side, no matter how ridiculous. I still miss eating whipped cream on the kitchen counter with you.

Quincey, for talking books, theology, and faith with me. I always come away from our conversations encouraged. Thanks for taking all our duplicate books. I like knowing they're in good hands.

Natalie, for being here when Felicity was born and being the aunt that Hadassah always goes to. You have a gift with the wee ones. If you ever are craving more chaotic childcare, I'm sure my daughters and I would be happy to accommodate.

Naomi and Noah, the two peas at the end, I love you guys. Thank you for making me smile and for playing "Colton and Sydney" on my wheelchair. It's good to know that I bring entertainment when I come, if nothing else.

Isaiah, my dear little brother, you're already with Jesus. I miss you. I love you always. I can't wait to see you again.

Heidi, a true friend, for naming my first cane and walking with me through the miserable months of deployment, coming out to visit, long phone calls through distance, life changes, and into motherhood. I miss you and wish you lived in the Idaho panhandle instead of the Florida one. But I will forgive you that.

Cheyenne, for being my book-writing partner from the beginning, and the first person I told about this little manuscript I swore would never see the world, who reminded me that this story was worth putting down on paper anyway. For still sharing your drafts with me through Google Docs like we did in good ol' England and Douglas Bond's Scriptorium. I love talking writing with you—and also life, motherhood, and all the little in-betweens.

Bo, from HawtPlate—the best restaurant in town. For your warm hospitality that first day in the parking lot when you were watering the flower baskets, and for keeping me going with hot coffee and cinnamon rolls so I could finish these last rounds of edits. Also for continually insisting on buying the first copy—I am definitely *giving* you one.

Lisa Leidenfrost, for your encouragement, wisdom, and practical counsel that was a saving grace to me during the deployment and in these years after. When I am sinking, you are the first person I think of to call. For pointing me to Jesus, making me aware of my own confusion of who I am and how deep God's grace goes in saving me.

You have been through the fire, and now you help people through theirs. I am so thankful for you.

Anna Edwards, for your prayers and presence that lifted me out of one of the darkest seasons of deployment. I still remember you holding my hands on my floor mattress in my studio, telling me that God was making me into a butterfly. Every conversation with you leaves me staggered by God's goodness and faithfulness, the beauty of this deep sorrow, the redemption you show in your life and heart, even when bleeding before the Lord. I weep with you, hope with you, look to Jesus with you.

My professors, who called me forward all the way to graduation and poured wisdom into both me and this book:

Dr. Edwards, for the numerous accommodations those last three years, for continually checking in and finding ways to make things easier, connecting me with people who could help, and for staying cool that picture day when I fainted in front of everyone and had a seizure.

Dr. Schlect, for pouring into me not only as a teacher but as a mentor. For pushing me to try the things I thought impossible, for being the final shove toward getting the wheelchair I desperately needed, for making that history field trip day the highlight of my sophomore year. My oral finals with you were a high point of my college experience, and I still get a thrill inside when someone mentions Thucydides.

Dr. Grieser, for believing in my writing while never failing to push me to be more poignant, more specific, and more beautiful with my words. For pouring into the early versions of this manuscript as my thesis advisor and professor, and going above and beyond with your careful edits and thoughtful suggestions. You kept the impostor syndrome at bay and made my thesis-writing experience deeply meaningful. I will always appreciate and admire your advice and counsel. Classes with you were a joy. Dostoevsky is now one of my favorites.

Dr. McIntosh, Mr. Griffith, and Dr. Stokes—for all the many

accommodations, last-minute changes, and flexibilities formerly unheard of. Your grace, encouragement, and faithfulness extended far beyond the classroom—and that is saying something, because classes with you were life-changing.

Kathleen, my agent and friend, for finding me and believing in this story from the first moment. For your continual emails and words of encouragement that always seemed to come at just the right time. For being the only professional partner I've ever sent GIFs to, for making me bring my toddler and newborn onto our business calls, and for so wholeheartedly rejoicing with me through the process of my first book. I am so thankful the Lord brought us together when He did—I can't imagine a better person to help bring this story to the world.

Lisa-Jo, my beloved editor. Your insight sharpened this book from day one. Again and again, your words drew out the best in my writing—and in me. Thank you for your patient flexibility, cheerful encouragement, and faithful recommendations. I loved working with you. You have been the very best editor (and friend) to walk with me through this long and meaningful process.

The teams at Alive and W Publishing, whose patience, brilliance, and care shaped these pages into something I could be proud of. Working with you has been pure joy.

Larry, Linda, and Sarah Ingalls, faithful friends and encouragers from the beginning. Thank you for your practical help, your hospitality, and your creative care when the future felt so uncertain. For setting up baby monitors in your guest room so I could stay a part of Bible study, for welcoming me into your home while Colton was away, and even finding a place for our kitten on the way back to Idaho. Your friendship, counsel, and encouragement carried me. I miss Charlie.

And finally, to everyone who has been part of this journey, seen or unseen: Your faithfulness, kindness, and prayers are woven into every word on these pages. Thank you for lifting my spirit and reminding me that even in brokenness, there is beauty, purpose, and grace.

notes

Chapter 1: Butterfly

1. Madeleine L'Engle, "Act III, Scene II," in *The Ordering of Love: The New and Collected Poems of Madeleine L'Engle* (Shaw Books, 2005), 55.
2. L'Engle, "Act III, Scene II," 55.
3. Leif Enger, *Peace Like a River* (Atlantic Monthly Press, 2001), 285.

Chapter 6: Disabled

1. Alan Noble, *On Getting Out of Bed: The Burden and Gift of Living* (InterVarsity Press, 2023), 51–52.
2. "Celebrating the International Day of Persons with Disabilities," Bournemouth University, December 3, 2022, https://microsites.bournemouth.ac.uk/student-blog/2022/12/03/celebrating-the-international-day-of-persons-with-disabilities.
3. Charles Wesley, "Christ the Lord Is Risen Today," Hymnary.org, accessed September 28, 2025, https://hymnary.org/text/christ_the_lord_is_risen_today_wesley.

Chapter 8: Burden

1. 1 Thessalonians 5:16–18.

Chapter 9: Belief

1. "A Life on Display," Joni and Friends, November 1, 2019, https://joniandfriends.org/1-minute-radio-program/a-life-on-display/.
2. C. S. Lewis, Mere Christianity (HarperOne, 2001), Book III, chapter 9.

Chapter 15: Lessons

1. C. S. Lewis, *Letters of C. S. Lewis*, ed. W.H. Lewis (Harcourt, 1966), 395.

Chapter 17: Together

1. The Westminster Standard, "The Kids' Catechism: An Introduction to the Shorter Catechism," questions 68 and 71, accessed April 23, 2025, https://thewestminsterstandard.org/the-kids-catechism/.

Chapter 18: Wings

1. John Milton, "Sonnet 19: When I Consider How My Light Is Spent," *Poetry Foundation*, accessed April 23, 2025, https://www.poetryfoundation.org/poems/44750/sonnet-19-when-i-consider-how-my-light-is-spent.
2. Milton, "Sonnet 19."
3. Milton, "Sonnet 19."
4. Milton, "Sonnet 19."
5. Psalm 23:1; Proverbs 3:5; Psalm 1:3; Isaiah 41:10; Philippians 4:7 NIV; John 3:16.

about the author

Sydney Anne Bennett is a writer and disability advocate. She helps people struggling with disability and chronic pain find confidence and hope again while pointing them to Jesus. She started sharing her story on Instagram two years ago, and her audience has since grown to over 285,000 followers.

Two weeks after her honeymoon, Sydney became disabled and was diagnosed with functional neurological disorder. This is a disorder of the amygdala, which controls pain/fear signals and fine motor function. Her brain sends the wrong signals to her central nervous system. This causes debilitating symptoms, including chronic pain, daily seizures, and loss of motor control that forces Sydney to use a wheelchair most of the time.

Learning to live with this disability, as well as the loss and pain that comes with it, has been one of her greatest struggles, and a way in which God is building strength. She actively documents her difficulties and triumphs through this illness. Her pain and hope are resonating with millions of readers across the world as she points to the Cross through the present brokenness of this world and her body.

Sydney currently lives in Idaho with her husband, Colton, and their sweet daughters, Hadassah and Felicity.

Connect with Sydney Anne Bennett

If Sydney's story has touched you, you're invited to follow along as she continues to share her journey.

With openness and vulnerability, Sydney writes about life, disability, and faith.

You are welcome to join her online community, whether you want to read more, find encouragement, or simply share in her journey.

For additional information, visit:

Instagram: @the.annegirl
Website: sydneyannebennett.com